ON THE ROAD WITH

DUTCH

MASON

David Bedford & Harvey Sawler

NIMBUS
PUBLISHING

Nimbus Publishing Limited
PO Box 9166, Halifax, NS   B3K 5M8
(902) 455-4286

Printed and bound in Canada

Design: Margaret Issenman

Front cover: On the steps of a Montreal walk-up in the late 1980s. Left to right: Paul Brown, Gary Blair, Ron Lepard, Gregg "Fish" Fancy and Rick Jeffery. Dutch is at centre.

Back cover: The band inside the story of *On The Road With Dutch Mason*, at Bearly's Bar and Grill in Halifax. Left to right: keyboardist Barry Cooke, bass player Charlie Phillips, guitarist Carter Chaplin, harp player David Bedford and drummer Ainsley "AJ" Jardine. Photo by Morrow Scot-Brown

David Bedford photo: Harvey Studios, Fredericton, NB
Harvey Sawler photo: Sharon French, Palm Springs, CA

Personal and family photos appear courtesy of Pam Mason.

Library and Archives Canada Cataloguing in Publication

Bedford, David, 1954-
On the road with Dutch Mason, Prime Minister of
the blues / David Bedford and Harvey Sawler.
ISBN 1-55109-510-6

1. Mason, Dutch. 2. Singers—Canada—Biography. 3. Guitarists—Canada—Biography. 4. Blues musicians—Canada—Biography. I. Sawler, Harvey, 1954- II. Title.

ML420.M399B42 2005   782.421643'092   C2005-900001-5

The Canada Council | Le Conseil des Arts
for the Arts | du Canada

Canadä

We acknowledge the financial support of the Government of Canada through the Book Publishing Industry Development Program (BPIDP) and the Canada Council for our publishing activities.

Dedicated to the many practitioners of the blues in the Maritimes and across Canada who over the years have played with and supported Dutch Mason.

ACKNOWLEDGEMENTS

The tour described in this book is ficticious. Everything else we believe to be true. There are a number of people who we must thank and whose assistance was indispensable. Foremost among these is Pam Mason, who graciously gave of her time and kindly gave us access to most of the photographs used in this book. Thanks to Amy Louie, Grossman's Tavern in Toronto; David Wham, the Rainbow Room in Ottawa; John Cavanagh, The Pond in Truro; Mimi at Bearly's Bar and Grill, Halifax; and Glenda M. Bishop, Kentville. Thanks also to the many blues men and women of the Maritimes who know and love Dutch and who were generous in sharing their stories and experiences. We greatly appreciate the guidance, patience, vision and humour of editor Sandra McIntyre. Thanks also to Sandra's Nimbus colleagues, Dan Soucoup, Heather Bryan, Helen Matheson, Terrilee Bulger, and Penelope Jackson. Finally, we must thank our life partners (to use a most unbluesy term), who listened to the endless whining and who tolerated the insufferable self-indulgence that inevitably accompanies any attempt, however modest, to be creative.

David Bedford and Harvey Sawler

CONTENTS

Red Hot Dutch

The city is Halifax, Nova Scotia; the time is the early 1970s. Asleep in bed, naked, is Dutch Mason, the Prime Minister of the Blues, the rising legend of the music scene in Canada.

His rest is disturbed by a slowly building, acrid smell. Secretly, silently, the room begins to fill with deadly smoke. Dutch suddenly awakens and, frightened by the impending disaster, he leaps to his feet and grabs for his precious guitar, thinking as he does of the famous story of his idol, B. B. King, who almost burned to death running back into a fire to rescue *the guitar*, which in the story's aftermath became known to the world as "Lucille." One step ahead of B. B., Dutch dashes out of the building, guitar in hand, to stand naked on the street staring in horror at his close encounter, amazed that he's escaped with his life and his guitar.

He pauses.

"Fuck!" he shouts. "Jesus fuckin' Christ!"

He's forgotten to wake his girlfriend, Virginia.

CHAPTER ONE

True Blues Dutch

That's life, that's what all the people say
Riding high in April, slow down in May
But I know I'm gonna change that tune
When I get back on top in June
That's life, funny as it may seem
Some people get their kicks stomping on a dream
But I don't let it get me down
Because this fine old world keeps spinning 'round.

"That's Life," Kelly Gordon

It was Dutch's bass player, Charlie Phillips, who told me the story of the fire. Thankfully, Virginia escaped unharmed, and Dutch eventually did find some clothes. I heard that he gave his precious guitar to a guy in Fredericton, some time after arthritis took its harsh toll on his once-electrifying fingers.

Dutch's world is so chaotic and unpredictable, so devoid of planning and order, that it's remarkable he is still alive at all. The pestilence, war, famine and death ascribed to the four horsemen in the Bible seem trivial compared to what Dutch has put himself through. As for me, I could never have predicted that I would wind up playing harp for

Dutch's eleven-city tour of Eastern Canada as a fill-in for Rick Jeffery—
my musical idol and inspiration. I felt bad taking Ricky's place. He had
been Dutch's harp player, right-hand man and close friend for thirty
years, but after undergoing a double lung transplant, Ricky wasn't
physically capable of doing the tour, and Dutch invited me to stand in.
The very thought that I'd be playing harp with Dutch on the road was
nothing short of astonishing.

I was no stranger to the blues and the harp, and I'd played the odd gig
with Dutch before, but the stories of blues musicians on the road—the
bars, the audiences, the all-nighters, hard drinking and camaraderie—
were to me nothing more than that: far-flung stories. I was a fifty-year-
old professor and family man living a suburban life, and what I knew of
the blues was almost purely academic, like how I see it as a culture unto
itself, with its own liturgy and high priests, sacraments and sacred texts.
My limited exposure to the blues had driven home the distance between
Dutch's world and my own. I teach political science at the University of
New Brunswick, while Dutch has never had any job other than music.
I represent the middle class, he the under class. I'm expected to be
proper and polite, where Dutch and the others in the band can be rude
and vulgar. I am repressed; they are free. My social behaviour masks
oppression; Dutch and the guys act and feel honestly. I plan, and Dutch
takes it as it comes.

To put it metaphorically, I vacuum my Camry out every week and
Dutch drives a big, old lumbering Caddy. I work out. He smokes. I
have a diversified retirement portfolio. He's blown all the money he's
ever earned on booze and cars and good times. I'm embarrassed about
anything to do with the body, and he prefers being naked no matter
who's around. I was so square in high school that when the guidance
counsellor issued an aptitude questionnaire, mine came back "priest."

Dutch, on the other hand, has never had to ask himself if he is the genuine article, the real deal. He has never needed an aptitude test to tell him who he is. He's lived the blues man's life as outsider and rebel, the voice of suffering and the redeemer of pain, since he was seventeen. He plays like a blues man and he lives, talks and acts like one. Whether you see him perform or talk to him after the show, you have no doubt about his authenticity.

Just as nothing makes a middle-aged man look and feel more silly and out of place than a girlfriend half his age, I had hoped that three weeks on the road with the Prime Minster of the Blues, the king of the road, the wildest of all the out-of-control musicians, wouldn't make me feel more staid and buttoned-down than I actually was. I did not want to be some Faust—a parody: ivory tower professor by day, wannabe blues star by night. The only way to find out was to dive in head first, adopt Dutch's "don't-give-a-shit" attitude and, as the Nike ads say, "just do it." I was scared, but at least I would know whether or not I really belonged. Bravely or unwittingly, like Henry David Thoreau committing himself to extracting the essence out of life at Walden Pond, I headed for the road, with Dutch Mason, the quintessential blues man, as my guide.

CHAPTER TWO

The Chaotic Order of the Blues

I'm going up the country, water tastes like wine
Jump in the river, stay drunk all the time
I'd rather drink muddy water, sleep in a hollow log
Than to be in Atlanta, treated like a dirty dog

"Goin' To Chicago," Count Basie/Jimmy Rushing

While everyone knows that the blues is all about *disorder*, I noticed even before the tour that there are also strange traces of order. Somehow, behind the drug, the blues kicking in, there is a definite structure to who leads in a blues band—who calls the shots, who directs things, who calls what tunes to play and in what order, who's "the big boss man," who takes and divvies up the pay and who calls the load-in times and rehearsals. So despite the fact that there are no musical charts and arrangements, the music happens nevertheless from some form of understanding or order—an unwritten contract among the band members that there will be patterning and uniformity, that it will all come out right.

5

In every band, there's also an order as to where each musician stands. It's different from one band to the next, but within every band, it's always the same. For Dutch Mason's band, it's Ainsley Jardine—AJ—on drums at centre rear, the standard spot for drums; me, Dave Bedford, to AJ's far right, with guitarist Carter Chaplin between us. Bass player Charlie Phillips is to AJ's immediate left, with keyboard player Barry Cooke on the far left. Front and centre of course is Dutch Mason himself.

Almost inexplicably, simply instinctively, this is what bands do. They establish a natural order, a formation. Once set, it is unwavering. Whatever else they might be debating—like set lists, where to order pizza after the gig or who didn't help with the load-in—you just don't see guys or ladies milling around on stage trying to decide who will stand where. Elton John with his piano far stage right. It's Paul on the left, George and Ringo centre and John on the far right. Orchestras with their tympani and percussion to the rear, the conductor at the podium and the strings, winds, brass, guitars and piano all in their normal places. Tony Bennett encircled by his longtime piano player Ralph Sharon, stand-up bass man Doug Richeson and drummer Clayton Cameron. Jim Morrison standing exactly where he belonged. It's not only regimental bands that are regimental.

Dutch's earlier bands all had their structures too, including the core group from his heyday; Dutch in the centre, backed by Garry Blair on drums, with Rick Jeffery playing harp to Dutch's right, organist Donny Muir beside Rick, Gregg "Fish" Fancy on bass to Dutch's left, and piano player John Lee on the far left. In the era of the Dutch Mason Trio, the 1960s, the structure was simpler but still constant, with Dutch on guitar and vocals on one side, Kenny Clattenburg on drums and Ronnie Miller on bass.

CHAPTER THREE

Dutch's Truro Apartment

Wednesday, November 5, 2003

I walked 47 miles of barbed wire,
Used a cobra snake for a neck tie.
Got a brand new house on the roadside,
Made out of rattlesnake hide.
I got a brand new chimney made on top,
Made out of human skulls.
Now come on darling let's take a little walk, tell me,
Who do you love,
Who do you love, Who do you love, Who do you love.

"Who Do You Love," Ellas McDaniel

It was Wednesday, November 5, and our first gig was scheduled for Friday night at Grossman's, the home of the blues in Toronto. I'd driven from Fredericton, getting to Dutch's place at ten to eleven, with coffees in hand from Tim Hortons. It might seem crazy to drive from Fredericton to Truro and then backtrack, but I'd decided I wanted to be with the guys from the start. Carter, Charlie and Barry were already there but, not surprisingly, there was no sign of AJ. Dutch was holding court, killing time entertaining us with his road stories. As was inevitable, the subject of Rick Jeffery came up.

Well, boys, that's too *f*'n bad about Ricky. They went and did all that shit to him, new body parts and like that. Two new lungs and what's the point. He still can't play. Can't hardly *f*'n breathe, so how could he play harp? So Carter, what the *f* did they say about him?

"He's just not recovering like other guys who had the same operation at the same time," said Carter. "They've all gotten back to normal—whatever normal is for guys with two new lungs—but with that infection he had after the operation, he's just never bounced back."

"It's a real drag Dutch," I said to Dutch, meaning to include Carter. Charlie and Barry had gone to the Mainway for cigarettes for Dutch. "I thought about him all the way up here on the highway. It feels weird going on the tour when he'd normally be here instead. Carter called me before I left and I talked about what he said with Sue and she says it doesn't look good for him at all. Not at all."

Oh yeah, Sue's a *f*'n doctor, right? Why would a good looking woman like that be with you? Oh, you know I'm just *f*'n kidding ya Dave.

"I know," I said, "but Sue will tell it like it is. Doctors do that. I feel kind of guilty hitting the road with you with Ricky back in Halifax because I know he'd love to be back out playing. That's all he's wanted since the operation. He told me before he went to Toronto that he didn't care if he died as long as he could blow even once more like he used to. If God has any mercy he'll get a chance to. But he does look sick."

Dave, he's looked like a *f*'n vampire for thirty *f*'n years.

"Yeah, like Bela Lugosi," I said. "Or that Christopher Walken look."

Oooh yeah, that's who Ricky is…the Christopher *f*'n Walken of the Blues.

❖ ❖ ❖ ❖

Dutch has a way with words. Especially one. He is the most consistent and inventive user of the expletive "fuck," certainly in the history of Atlantic Canada. It dominates his language and his dialogue with such prominence and repetitiveness that it no longer resembles a swear word. It occupies every possible syntactic role and has so many nuances that it would be hard to catalogue them all.

The constant presence of the word is disconcerting, but it is a pattern, an unconventional convention that one can get caught up in immediately. Interestingly, the guys in the band swear much more around Dutch or when telling stories about him, because he is our leader and the role model for our world. If I swore more after a single night's gig with Dutch and the band, you can just imagine what I sounded like after three weeks. Swearing, and in particular the use of the "f" word, is part of life on the road. With Dutch, though, it's, excuse me, beyond all fucking reason.

❖ ❖ ❖ ❖

"Even knowing we were going to be away for the better part of three weeks," I said to Dutch, "Sue was great about it. She also didn't say a thing about me being away a good part of last weekend on top of doing the tour."

What a ƒ'n doll she is.

"You're right. Thanks."

What the ƒ do you mean, "thanks." I said "Sue" was a doll. Anyway, where the ƒ is AJ? What ƒ'n time is it anyway Dave?

"Almost one."

He knew he was supposed to be here by eleven o'clock. Even Ricky when he was real ƒ'n sick would show up on time, but not ƒ'n AJ. I'm going to ƒ'n kill AJ, if he ever gets here.

Speaking of death, you know when I was doing all that shit to myself, like Ricky was doing although I never did the drugs like he did, I had no idea what the ƒ it was going to do to my health. All I knew was that I was playing. I didn't sit around and say—"Well, I better take a couple of vitamin B's, I have to play to ƒ'n two in the morning, maybe I better take my C's" and, you know. I just ƒ'n played and went along with it. So imagine Ricky, all the stuff he put his body through.

We all love to hear the stories of Dutch and his bands and their days of being out of control while on the road. There is still envy and nostalgia for the days when the inmates ran the asylum—we cheer when Jack Nicholson first takes control of matters in *One Flew Over The Cuckoo's Nest*. No wonder we keep prompting Dutch to talk about the old days just one more time.

"So, what exactly was he doing out there Dutch?"

He was nuts, just *f*'n nuts you know. There was one time that AJ told me about. Ricky, Terry Edmonds and AJ were in their hotel room somewhere, I forget where. Now back in those days they had the hotel rooms with the ceilings that had the water pipes outside the ceilings, right, so Terry and AJ had these two girls there and they had a forty-ouncer of vodka sitting in between their two beds on the dresser. So this vodka was sitting there and all of a sudden, they're there talking, and Ricky comes knocking at the door. He comes walking in and he's got just his underwear on. And Terry and AJ got these two girls and they tell him—"Ricky, we got these two women here, would you get out?" He says—"No, no come on." He's drinking, right. I told you about his drinking, eh, Dave. So he walks in and he takes a great big swig out of the vodka—"Come on, come on, you guys let me have a drink." They're going "Ooohhh!" So he takes a drink of the vodka and puts it back down, so they start talking again. Like Terry and AJ are smoking a joint, you know, just marijuana and that and having drinks and they're talking to the girls, not thinking anything, got the music going.

All of a sudden Ricky jumps up in the air and grabs those water pipes that go across the ceiling, so he starts shimmying across the ceiling, going across and they're looking up going—"What the *f* is this guy doing?"—So he's going across and AJ says—"Ricky, get the fuck down." So he grabs Ricky by the underwear and pulls him. He comes crashing down, smashes the vodka bottle, the whole forty-ouncer of liquor that Terry and AJ just got, smashes that all over the place, he's all cut, he's got all these little cuts all over him and he's laying on the floor, so Terry grabs him by the arms and AJ grabs him by the feet and they drag him from their room all the way up the hallway, which was about ten rooms up and then down the other hallway, which is another ten rooms, on the carpet, on the floor.

He wakes up the next day and he's got carpet burns, he's got rips in his arse and all over his back and until a year or two later, he still had scars from these carpet burns, which ripped all his arse open and his legs and his knees.

"It's hard to believe that you guys lasted all those years. Or that you didn't wind up killing one another."

If he was on dope, he was *f*'n fine, but once he got on the booze, he was a *f*'n maniac. The booze just made him like an animal.

"Yeah," I said to Dutch. Carter and Charlie came through the door with Dutch's smokes. "Ricky told me about that once and he thought it was funny."

And apparently he kept coming back down. He'd wake up and they'd drag him and throw him in the room. They'd come running back down the hall again, drag him back up and he started chasing Terry with the—well, he actually grabbed the vodka bottle. He comes in and starts chasing Terry all over the hotel with this broken vodka bottle, trying to kill him. Trying to kill him with that.

But to finish the story, when Rick was in the hospital in the summer, AJ reminded him of that story earlier this year. He was joking around with him. He showed AJ his scar on his stomach and AJ said—"Ricky, that's almost as big as the one you had on your arse." He just laughed his head off. That was one of the biggest jokes.

"He's just as insane about money," said Carter, prompting Dutch.

Jeez, I f'n guess. I remember these phone calls in Yellowknife he kept on putting on, calling his baby back home and he gets—what—a $700 bill. The government called from down there in Halifax and said to take all his money off him and pay it back to them. At the end of the two weeks we were up there, he had a paycheck of about $160.

Yeah, he had no money at all. So now Ricky never bought a steak in his life. Ricky never bought any f'n thing that was any more than a sandwich or something. And one time AJ said—"Ricky, look, I'll vouch for you. Don't worry, I'll buy your meals and stuff." All of a sudden everybody sees these porterhouse steaks and f'n mushrooms and escargots and f'n shrimp cocktails, and AJ's going—"Hold on a f'n minute,"—he said, holy fuck. And AJ's buying him these extravagant f'n meals, you know what I mean. That's what he used to do.

"Not a good guy to place on an open-ended expense account, you're saying, Dutch?"

Jeez Dave, are ya f'n crazy. There was this guy—we used to call him Deputy Dog. We were at the end of the second week and we'd been eating in this restaurant. Anyway he told us by the end of the second week we were there, he said—"You know the waitresses and that were wondering why you guys are so cheap…" We go—"What do you mean, so cheap?" He said—"Well, you guys are here every day of the week and you get paid and you're making money and—even the Indians, they tip—but you guys aren't tipping anybody in there, serving you guys and all the girls are just…." And AJ and the guys are going—"What? We always leave big tips. Dutchie always leaves a five dollar tip every time he goes." What it was, we'd all eat and Ricky would be the last one at the table and he'd say—"Oh I'm just going to eat," because he always liked grizzle off the pork chops. He'd say— "Listen, can I have yours?" you know, before he'd even order, before he had to pay his money out, he'd see what we were ordering first, to make sure he might be able to get a meal out of it before he had to pay his money out. He had no money because of the phone bills because he was always calling his woman back home in Nova Scotia. So what ended up happening was that Ricky would stay at the table to say he was eating our grizzle and he'd finish up our meals, the leftovers, and he'd take all the tips.

He'd take all the tips we'd leave and that way he had more money than us by the end of the two weeks. I always left five dollars, automatically five dollars, and all the money was gone, eh. That's why he got nicknamed the Finance Minister of the Blues.

❊ ❊ ❊ ❊

If Dutch is the most singular and talented person I've ever met, Rick was the most unusual, at once charming and hard, sensitive and extraordinarily vulgar, thoughtful and crooked, as Dutch can well attest. Rick always made me laugh too. He had a funny bumper sticker on the back of one of his amps—a friend got it for him at Roswell, New Mexico, where some say the U. S. government found an alien spaceship that crashed. It read: "I like aliens—they taste like chicken."

Like the others, I couldn't get enough of Dutch's early days, even though listening to him is like a verbal jigsaw puzzle; band members and their wives leaving and arriving, except for AJ, who among this crowd has been with Dutch the longest. That's the AJ who it seems was *not arriving.* He was really late by then, more than three hours. Which meant he either couldn't find his drums, or he slept in, or he was watching TV, or he missed his drive, or whatever. Even Dutch was getting really antsy. Carter's ten-year-old Nissan pickup and Dutch's '95 El Dorado Cadillac were sitting on the street in this quiet neighbourhood in Truro, Nova Scotia. The vehicles were full of gas and gear and tattered luggage. Not much more than tote sacks. My bag, on the other hand, was nearly new. Inside it, everything was orderly and in its place, as though it were packed by a librarian or a chartered accountant.

We were waiting for AJ in the small addition Dutch rents on the back of a house that fronts on Muir and sides on Arlington Street.

Just making small talk, I asked Dutch whether it ever occurred to him that the street he lived on was a namesake to his former keyboard player, Donny Muir.

Well, what the *f* are you thinkin' Dave? But don't go telling Donny they named a street after him. He'll tell the guys and they'll all want a street in Truro named after them.

"You mean like AJ Avenue?"

Oh could you just *f*'n imagine. You would never hear the end of it. Whatever street, it would end up being a never-ending rotary. And he'd be late for his own *f*'n ribbon-cutting.

Dutch lives in this place with two others guys who are in what, in cruel irony, we call "the golden years," the three of them subsisting on disability payments, except for the money Dutch makes from the odd gig. The small addition to the house is so cramped that it defies logic how the three of them survive. Forget their simultaneous, incessant smoking and the fact that they won't open the windows because they say it's too cold outside. The entire quarters is so cramped—kitchen, a bed, a recliner, Dutch's wheelchair, a couple of extra places to sit, plus a bathroom—the entire living space is probably equal to one of Bill Gates' bathrooms.

Dutch lives in his bed. He's naked most of the time. Wade Brown lives in the recliner, which actually butts up against the end of Dutch's bed. Tiny Kennedy lives in Dutch's wheelchair, which is just inches from Dutch's bed. When Dutch needs the wheelchair, Tiny has to go sit in the kitchen—either that or hope Wade goes out somewhere.

✺ ✺ ✺ ✺

We had two days to get to Toronto. Not that Hogtown is *that* far away for anyone who'd get in their car and drive straight there, even over-nighting along the way. But this bunch wasn't just any bunch. I'd never really toured with these guys before, but I'd done enough gigs with them to have the overwhelming sense that some catastrophe could happen at any time. I knew that any number of things could slow our forward progress, and I'm not talking about gridlock on the 401. There was Dutch, bass player Charlie Phillips, guitarist Carter Chaplin, keyboardist Barry Cooke, AJ—that is, supposing AJ was actually coming—and me, and three weeks of gigs.

If we're goin' to get on the *f*'n road, let's get on the *f*'n road. I can't even move my *f*'n fingers and I'm here and ready. Where the *f*'s AJ?

The two worst ones for it were Garry Blair and Ronnie Miller because they were always whacked out on junk, eh, so they didn't give

a *f* if they made the job or not I guess. I don't know what they thought. But I'd be psyching myself up three hours before the job just to *f*'n, to get myself in a mental *f*'n stage where I could play—humming tunes and you know. It was weird.

Dutch was lighting one Marlboro after another. I thought I was going to choke to death. Carter, who was sitting at the kitchen table, was slouched so that his legs were stretched out across part of the floor. Barry was just listening, minding his own business. They've all spent more time on the road with Dutch and have heard his stories over and over to the point where they can tell them—hence Charlie's telling me about the story of the fire, Dutch's narrow naked escape and the leaving behind of Virginia. I still have the excited interest of the soon-to-be-initiated, listening carefully to the liturgy.

"So why keep playing with guys like that if they were always doing these things to you?"

Because we were friends and it's the worst *f*'n thing to do in a band is to be friends with the guys in the bands. You can be friends at a distance, like you know what I mean. We're friends, right, you and me, but we can't be too close a *f*'n friend because then all of a sudden—"Well, I'm your *f*'n buddy, I was here, blah, blah, blah"—and then it's like that, it's a personal *f*'n fight whenever something goes wrong. If you have friends that come in and play like that, you let them *f*'n know that you're the leader of the band and if they *f* up, they're gone. That's the way a band should be, which I never did that. It was my own *f*'n fault.

A small voice inside of me wanted to ask Dutch if we're friends. Wisely, I told it to shut the *f* up.

CHAPTER FOUR

Still in Dutch's Apartment

I woke up this mornin', feelin' 'round for my shoes,
Know by that I got these mean old walking blues.
Well, leave this morning if I have to, ride the blind,
I feel mistreated and I don't mind dyin'.

"Walkin' Blues," Robert Johnson

So where the *f* is *f*'n AJ?

Dutch was really getting impatient.

Dave, how about going to the store and getting us something to eat?

Dutch knew that the answer concerning AJ's whereabouts could be any number of things. Dutch, Carter, Charlie, Barry and I, we all knew. The fact that we were waiting for AJ to come from Halifax for nearly four hours was not news. We were aware of this tendency of his. No, not "tendency." It's more like a trait, or a characteristic, or a quality, using the word very loosely. So why the *f* did the rest of us arrive at Dutch's on time anyway? It struck me though, that in his own way, AJ is actually one hundred per cent reliable. Late, but predictably so, thereby doing his small part to keep the world comfortably on its axis, the universe on course.

This is what every one of us who knows AJ knows: That being late probably had to do with Ellen's cats. He either had to walk them, feed them, take them to the vet, find one that had run away or perhaps wait while one gave birth. Or it might have had to do with his kit, which he had to get from Bearly's, but he had no car and expected someone to drive him who didn't show up—or he forgot to ask them in the first place. Or the drums were in hock somewhere. Or he had to go to a physio appointment or take a cab downtown to pay his rent, or he was at Ellen's parents' place for the weekend and was late getting back into Halifax. Or he just slept in. Or he didn't have bus fare, or he had something on the stove, or no one picked him up to go to the bank to cash a cheque because the bar paid him with a cheque instead of cash and he doesn't have a bank account so he had to wait until the bank opened to cash the cheque and no one was around to drive him except maybe Ellen's father and he—Ellen's father—had to go to the hardware store first and then fix his tap and by then the bank was closed, so AJ had to wait until the next day to get the guys in the band their money. When he eventually did show up, AJ would likely say: "It's really not my fault and Dave, you really shouldn't be so unreasonable, okay!"

Dutch told me one night, early on in my sojourn with his band—a night when AJ was late arriving for a gig at the Bugaboo in Fredericton—what it can be like dealing with his drummer.

Garrett [Dutch's son] and I have talked about, well, just trying to get AJ organized for a gig, Dave. I mean this is one guy to try and get organized and it's just impossible. It really is. I want this, can I have

that. I want to go here. I have to go there. Ellen's going over to her sister's place. I might be able to get a car from so-and-so. So many f'n stories that at the end you just f'n say—"See you"—and hang up the phone. What can you f'n say? He says—"Everything is fine, don't worry about nothing"—but you know everything is not fine—"You're an idiot." But AJ's a good man on the road. He's a good f'n road guy and he's an excellent f'n drummer. He always did real good with money and I let him look after the f'n money and that. I just said— "Here, you look after the fuckin' money. I'll be too drunk to ever split it up." And that's the way that went.

There is a reason why some people are accountants or managers or professors and some people play drums for a living. You don't get to be that good a blues drummer by being punctual with your homework assignments in school, which is probably why we were sitting in Dutch's Truro apartment waiting for AJ for what seemed an eternity. Waiting for AJ was like waiting for Godot. I told Dutch of the time we were playing a showcase gig at the East Coast Music Awards in Saint John, in 2002. AJ came up to me and asked where his drums were.

"How should I know?" I said.

"Well, you know I don't have a car and you knew the drums were in my room, so I just assumed you'd take them for me. You'd better hurry if you're going to get them in time." He said this with a hint of impatience in his voice, just enough to show me that although I had screwed up, *he* was trying to be understanding about it. I almost killed him that night.

Sitting in Dutch's room, trying to get a breath through the clouds of cigarette smoke, I began to think about the blues, about why someone like Dutch or AJ would devote their whole life to it. More than anything else the blues is about rebellion, which incorporates all the rest—bedlam, mayhem, chaos and disorder. It is a rebellion against the established social hierarchies that privilege one class in society and oppress another. Rebellion against the pain that the inescapable facts of life and death bring to everyone in the end. Rebellion against the suffering of the heart that might not be as inevitable as death but is just about as common and often more terrible. Rebellion against the indignity of hard work that is paid back with poverty and despair.

The great blues musicians who have created the idioms and themes of the genre—Muddy Waters and Robert Johnson, T-Bone Walker and Howlin' Wolf, Leadbelly and Sonny Terry—articulated their experiences, and those of their audience, in a music that is at once a lament against pain and a celebration of the joy of endurance and survival. They were outsiders from the established society. They and their audience experienced the American dream as an unending cycle of labour and debt, of sharecropping and migration to the slums of the northern cities, of being the victim of brutality while being portrayed as its perpetrators.

Folk music of various kinds emerges from local conditions and cultures, which is part of what makes blues a folk music. Blues came from the lives and suffering of the African American sharecroppers of the South following the Civil War. Dutch and the guys regard blues as black man's music, but they don't spend much time thinking about it. Except Carter. He pays a lot of attention to the music's history.

Blues is a legacy from the lives that sharecroppers led from the turn of the century, through their migration to the factories and inner cities of the north. The music itself is sad and full of regret, but it's also joyous and a spit in the eye of those who would degrade the lower class. The blues attracts because life can be monotonous. It is extravagant because life can be miserly. Above all, blues is the release from pain that cannot be faced.

Dutch is regarded as one of the great blues musicians. Everywhere I go I run into people who have memories of seeing him play. In a strange, distant sort of parallel to the sharecroppers' blues legacy, these are people who were and are attracted to, and moved by, the beat and pulse of the music. They can recall how, for at least a moment, everything could suddenly be fine. Life felt as though it would all turn out right. They remember their friends and the drinks and being free of care. Talking to people about Dutch opens me up to their world, to what it was like to be them ten or twenty or thirty years ago. No one is ever sad reminiscing about seeing the Dutch Mason Blues Band.

❖ ❖ ❖ ❖

My favourite book has always been *Huck Finn*. Hemingway called Mark Twain's classic the first true American novel. It is thought by many to be one of the first American books to tackle real sociological problems, including racism, slavery, domestic abuse and alcoholism. It was one of the first American books containing real speech characterizations. It was also the first book to raise the question of what was happening to the American Dream.

I see myself as Huck, and Dutch's big white Caddy as the raft wafting its way down the Mississippi. On this raft, as in the bars and hotel rooms of the road, the norms of society are gone. Huck yearns for the territories, a mythic place of freedom and salvation. I don't have such a place to go to, but I do have Dutch. When people are with him, they are guided by him, living without inhibition and outside of what we think of as civilization. Not a life lived more properly or better, but surely more naturally. Dutch is the ring leader and our inspiration. He doesn't ask us to behave this way. We just do it because that is how he acts and lives and we all look up to him. Dutch is the kind of person that my mother used to warn me to stay away from because he'd be a bad influence. Sorry mom, but I wish I hadn't had to wait until I was forty to meet him, because man, he is cool. Just knowing him is the coolest thing I've ever done. By a mile.

❋ ❋ ❋ ❋

As I returned from KFC with a bucket of chicken and rolls, AJ pulled up beside Dutch's place on Arlington Street. I parked my Camry back in the driveway, and AJ was transferring the jumble of parts resembling a drum kit from the trunk of his friend's car. Thrown into the trunk, AJ's drums looked as though they had exploded after the previous night's gig, or as though he'd carried out a finale befitting Keith Moon's antics with The Who. They always look this way, yet at every gig, he can still assemble all the errant and disheveled parts, like that TV show where a group of machinists and engineers are given twelve hours to make an airplane or water cannon using junk they find in a scrap yard. As the saying goes—if you want to enjoy the meal, don't look in the kitchen.

It was quarter to four, not eleven in the morning like it was supposed to be, and AJ was more anxious about our departure than apologetic about his belated appearance.

"Jesus AJ, Dutch is getting worried. Where the *f* have you been?"

"What are you talking about Dave? What's your friggin' problem? Dutch'll be fine. Totally fine."

He began with the usual litany of rationales as I walked up the small wheelchair ramp to Dutch's apartment entrance. It drove me nuts that no one was saying a word to AJ about being late. Dutch was suddenly in fine spirits, especially toward AJ. It was as though he'd not been the least bit late. I already looked like the anal ass, and we hadn't even left Arlington Street.

We consumed the chicken, with AJ tackling the greater share of the fifteen-piece bucket, got into the cars and turned right onto Prince Street, a one-way thoroughfare that cuts through Truro, left up to Queen and headed for Robie and the Trans-Canada Highway. AJ took the wheel of Dutch's Cadillac, with Dutch in the front and me in the back. Carter, Barry and Charlie took the truck. We were on our way.

CHAPTER FIVE

The TCH, Somewhere in New Brunswick

There ain't nothin' I can do, nor nothin' I can say,
that folks don't criticize me;
But I'm goin' to do just as I want anyway, I don't care if they all despise me.
If I should take a notion, to jump into the ocean,
It ain't nobody's business if I do.

"Ain't Nobody's Business," P. Grainger/E. Robbins

Even with us listening to blues and country and western CDs, the monotony of uncomplicated four-lane highways provided lots of time for talk. We spent a good deal of time playing and replaying conversations and the same old jokes, like the senseless banter of kids or the way Ed McMahon and Johnny Carson would do the same repetitive "Whooooa!" or "Yeeeoo!" every night whenever a joke went bad. I would put my head between the Caddy's front seats and try to get AJ going.

"Now sit back and be a good little boy," he warned me parentally.

"Jeez AJ, are we there yet?" I toyed with him, drawing out the letters of his name: "Aaaiii Jaaayyy."

"Sure Dave. Is this the kind of shit Sue has to put up with?"

And so it would go for the duration of the tour. Dutch would just tolerate us or tell us to *shut the f up* when he would listen to us at all.

❊ ❊ ❊ ❊

Being on the road was, in a sense, like going on the quintessential American adventure, for no one can deny that the blues experience is thoroughly American. The guitars and the amps are American; the cars are American; the clothes and music and heroes, the bar themes and food are all American. Of course, it's really more mythically or symbolically American—the majority of America is like me, more middle-class than rebel. But, in our romantic imaginations the experience is all Johnny Cash: cool guys dressed in black, hanging out at juke joints and biker bars, playing rockabilly and the blues.

I began to wonder how a kid from Lunenburg, Nova Scotia, went from doing the stereotypical thing of his era—forming a garage band playing Carl Perkins and Elvis and Jerry Lee Lewis—to becoming Canada's most renowned blues artist. There wasn't exactly a lot of sharecropping that went on in Dutch's early life. He swears, in fact, that being from Lunenburg, where everyone was pretty WASP in those days, he never even saw a black person until he was eleven years old. Yet eventually he ended up sitting in B. B. King's dressing room and sharing a playbill in Montreal as the only white performer among an entourage of legendary black blues performers.

❊ ❊ ❊ ❊

We stopped in Edmundston, just before the Quebec border. Between the two vehicles, we visited four different drive-thrus, finally stopping at an Irving with a large, country-style restaurant where we got gas and Dutch got an order of scallops to go.

You can hardly go wrong at an Irving gas station restaurant if you're looking for something that don't taste like ƒ'n fast food.

AJ wanted Wendy's, Carter wanted a Big Mac, Charlie and Barry each ordered a Tim Hortons coffee and tuna sandwich. I got a Subway cold cut on Parmesan Oregano bread.

We downed the grub with Dutch complaining both that he didn't have enough tartar sauce and that it was hard to eat scallops on his lap in the car. It was nearly eleven o'clock at night and the later it got, the more talkative Dutch became. He was talking about all the great blues performers he had played with, about how he got his nickname…

"So Dutch," I asked, "is it true B. B. King gave you the name Prime Minister of the Blues?"

Well, B. B. King is my ƒ'n idol you know. So once when I was playing at the Colonial in Montreal, I went in, B. B. was playing and they said, there's somebody upstairs wants to see you. And I said—"I want to stay here"—and Mike Lyons, the guy that owns the place said—"No, come upstairs, somebody up there wants to see you." So I went up the ƒ'n elevator, opened the door and there's B. B. King. So I didn't know what the ƒ to say, you know. So we talked about a half hour, like that, and he went down and went on stage and he was introduced and he's saying there's another blues band here tonight and blah, blah, blah and putting down his rap. There was a couple of black guys in front of me,

and one said, "Muddy Waters must be here tonight," like that, and then B. B. said my *f*'n name and the light came on me and I couldn't get to my *f*'n guitar. It was in the car about three blocks *f*'n away—it was in the winter time eh and *f*—I missed it, my chance to play with him.

But I did get to open for him in Montreal at Place des Arts there. It was back when they had just started the jazz festival in Montreal. I don't know the year although I would if I had the poster around. I was the only white guy in the whole *f*'n thing. I don't remember who the *f* else was there—*f*—anyway, they were all black guys. All black people and I was the only white guy. Wait a minute. Yeah, I think there was B. B., there was John Lee Hooker, Eddie "Cleanhead" Vinson, Clifton Chenier, Big Mama Thornton, Lightning Hopkins, Oscar Peterson, and this white guy—me.

That's when he called me the king of the blues for Canada but Ricky *f*'n said—"No, you should be called the Prime Minster of the Blues because we're in Canada." And I said—"That's a good idea."

I also played with Buddy Guy's band at the Colonial and yeah, he had on a plaid suit so I got up to play with him, like that, and he just walked over to the *f*'n bar and I could see him looking in the mirror when I started to play and then he turned around like that. The bar was all full of pimps and hookers and that. They were all clapping, you know, and he probably figured, white *f*'n boys can't playing nothing, you know. And I played like that and jeez, he had a terrible *f*'n band. I think he hired them. I don't know where the *f* he hired them. What a rotten *f*'n band he had. But Buddy himself is a great *f*'n singer. But every time with the guitar, he wasn't real hot on the guitar, you know, and we played for James Cotton a lot. We open for him in different places and he always had a good band.

I'll tell you one good *f*'n thing about James Cotton that will knock your socks off. This is *f*'n something else. We're in the back room, we're playing the Misty Moon—that's when it was out on the Camp Road—and there was our band and Cotton's band playing, right, two bands like, and we were playing there that night and we were just *f*'n loaded and I mean loaded and when I'm *f*'n loaded drunk, it takes a lot of liquor, and he can drink as much as me the *f*'n crazy *f*'er, eh, plus he smokes joints the size of Long John Holmes' dick, you know what I mean. So anyway, they're all going out the door and I said— "Fuck, I'm getting a cab." I ain't getting nailed for *f*'n driving my car even in town. Even back to the city, you know.

So I looked over and there's Cotton behind the *f*'n steering wheel and I went—"Where the fuck are you going?"—and he said— "Philadelphia"—and just started up the car and drove away. I couldn't believe it. What a good guy he is though, just a *f*'n great guy. But the guy is a little piss proud, like you know.

We played a lot with Cotton. They used to come in and when we played Newfoundland, they took two extra days off, even if they were going to *f*'n Alabama or some *f*'n thing and they didn't even bother to go. They just stayed over there with us a couple of days and jammed with us like you know. They said—"Cancel out the other *f*'n jobs and stay over here with Dutch and we'll party."

We used to drink together all the time. And them guys smoked a lot of dope, like hash and grass, you know, but I can't smoke that *f*'n stuff. If I smoke a *f*'n joint, your name would be Harvey or some *f*'n thing and I'd think you were a large rabbit, you know what I mean.

But we played with Cotton at the Misty Moon, at the Rising Sun in Montreal, we played Newfoundland with them, we played Calgary, Edmonton, all over the *f*'n place.

❊ ❊ ❊ ❊

Dutch has never wavered from playing blues. He started playing rockabilly, a variant of blues that evolved from the mixture of blues with bluegrass, the music indigenous to the largely white and poor Appalachian region. By the mid 1960s his feet were firmly planted in the musical soil of the rural south. When B. B. King heard him play, he wanted to know what part of Texas he was from. Dutch should have told him just for a joke that he was from Lunenburg, Texas, which is just outside of Austin. He has taken the stage as an equal with some of the very best blues performers to have ever played: B. B. King, James Cotton, Buddy Guy, Junior Wells, John Lee Hooker and many, many more. During the 1960s and 70s, when Dutch's bands toured constantly, blues was the heart and soul of popular music. Bands like the Rolling Stones, Led Zeppelin, Jimi Hendrix and Cream were playing the blues as the core of their sound. Being in a blues band was easier then if only because work was steadier and the pay was better. Plus, the outsider status of the blues genre had greater appeal then. The Reagan revolution, and the backlash against the civil rights, feminist and labour movements helped usher in popular forms of music that are more acceptable to middle-class society, one might say more antiseptic, than the blues.

But through all the changes in musical fashion, Dutch has kept play-ing the blues. Jobs are a lot harder to come by now and the pay isn't as good, but even if the audiences are smaller, they still respond to "Sweet Little Angel" or "Goin' To Chicago" as if they were hearing these songs for the first time.

Blues songs, like Dutch, are cool, not straight; sensual and dirty, not proper and clean. The rhythms and lyrics of blues songs are dark and subversive. When you hear Muddy Waters or Dutch Mason scream "I'm A Man," the time-clock-punching, income-tax-filing, cholester-ol-watching, mortgage-paying person is granted a release, a day pass to musical freedom. When the gig is over, they return to their normal selves. You can see in every audience a mixture of executives and secretaries, lawyers and plumbers, middle-aged couples and students. When the music's *on* and it's affecting them, you can sense them digging deep to find the blues. This is where the blues artist already resides.

Rick Jeffery once told me that you can tell you've played the truth when half the audience gets up and leaves, and the other half loves it. When that happens the music is not just entertainment, not just a piece of candy that tastes good momentarily—like bubble gum music, which does nothing for the soul. You have made a statement. When that happens, you have said something true and real.

❀ ❀ ❀ ❀

Somewhere between Edmundston and Notre-dame-du-lac in Quebec, I asked AJ again from over the back seat: "How long now Aaaaiii Jaaayyy?"

"Shut the *f* up Daaaave!"

Jokingly cast aside by AJ, I directed my banter to Dutch instead.

"So who else did you play with Dutch? What about Bo Diddley? Didn't you play with him?"

Yeah, I loved Bo Diddley. And Diddley is illiterate as *f*, eh. He's just not too brilliant and he's a good *f*'n guy, but he's not too smart. Like he'll take a word that has nothing to do with anything, like strictly confidential, he'll put it in a sentence like that. Now Bo Diddley is exactly ten years older than me and we were the obvious *f*'n band to play with him in Moncton and so they hired us to back him up and he didn't like the band at all. He hated our *f*'n band. He had us fired after

the second night. But the boys, the people I knew from Moncton in the crowd, were yelling—"Get that nigger off the stage and let Dutch play." So I think that had something to do with it.

So then he hired a band from Fredericton to back him up and he said it was the best group he ever worked with in his *f*'n life. So what the *f* is that? You're thinking to yourself, but he's not. See we wanted to find out about guys like Little Walter and who the *f* he played with and where they started at and what he was doing and how did he write that song.

Every time you'd start a *f*'n story with Bo Diddley, he'd say—"Yeah, Chuck Berry and I started it all"—you know what I mean. And we were saying—"Yeah, well we like Chuck Berry and that's fine"—and then we'd say—"Oh yeah, what about when you were playing with Little Walter?"—like that. He said—"Yeah, Little Walter is doing really good. He got a restaurant down in Florida." He was dead for ten *f*'n years! So you knew there was something wrong. Anyway, he's not too *f*'n sharp, you know. But I liked him anyway. And I used to sneak out before the *f*'n set started, like a half hour, and tune up his guitar and I would tune it up and put it back on the *f*'n stand. He'd come out and untune the whole *f*'n thing again and start playing. Like it was just *f*'n stupid. He was, I mean he still is a funny guitar player, like he doesn't really do much on the guitar.

"What about Muddy Waters?" I asked. "I saw him once, in 1975, with Pinetop Perkins on piano and Jerry Portnoy on harp."

I never played with Muddy Waters. I never did. I used to see him every night. We'd get in the elevator at the same time, but I've never seen him play in my life. Never. Just got in the elevator at the same time every night. Went downstairs—"See you Muddy"—"See you Dutch"—and away we went. He was at the Colonial and I was outside of town in the Queensbury Arms, so that's how I didn't get to *f*'n see him.

I played with Junior Wells in Montreal, at the Rising Sun and Buddy Guy was on stage, right. They must have hired these *f*'n musicians from the loading docks in New York City, down at the pipefitters club or something because they were *f*'n bad, eh, and Buddy's up there singing and he's introducing Junior. This goes on for twenty *f*'n minutes, he's introducing him. I said—"Junior, you got to get up there and sing some *f*'n thing." He said—"Fuck him. He owes me forty dollars from Detroit, he ain't paid me yet from that Checkers *f*'n joint." I said—"Junior, I'll go up and play with you." "All right, let's go up," he says. That's how it went. But Junior was a good *f*'n guy. He was a good guy. It was just that he was sick. He was *f*'n sick. And you know what it's like if you're roaming around and you can't breathe and you're playing harp like Ricky did, like *f* man, that's got to be the worst. So anyway, that was like my deal with Junior Wells.

But Junior was quite a *f*'n guy, eh. Ricky just loved him. Just *f*'n loved him. I liked Junior. I just liked the way he was a character, you know, and that's what you're looking for in this *f*'n business, characters, you know. But jeez, Ricky didn't get along with Buddy too well. They didn't get along at all. Now Buddy might *f*'n say—"I got along with him perfect" because you should never say anything about another *f*'n musician. The only reason I'll say it is because it's the *f*'n truth.

Hey Dave, how about this story. I was playing in Hamilton and I must have been twenty. And that's where I met John Lee Hooker. You got to hear this. I was playing in Hamilton, right, and it was a place called The Downstairs Club and I was playing across the street at the Flamingo, right, so I went across the street to the Downstairs Club because they were playing blues there, right. So you went downstairs and everything, and I'll tell who was playing there was Gordon Lightfoot. He was *f*'n playing. They were like the house people or whatever the *f* it was. And they were singing all kinds of, it had nothing to do with Gordon Lightfoot, he was just singing other stuff. I went over this night right and I went in the bathroom, now I had on a black *f*'n suit with red lining in it and I looked like one of the Mafia, you know, the hair all back like that. I looked like I was one of the *f*'n wise guys or something and I went in the bathroom and an old black guy walked in and he said— "Where can I get in touch with the black market?" I said—"What?" He said—"Where can I get in touch with the black market?" I said—"What do you want from the black market?" like that. He said—"I got to get a bottle of Scotch." I said—"Oh, I can get you a bottle of Scotch." Then he told me who he was. I said—"Oh fuck, how are you?"

So I went back across to my club, back across the street, got a bottle of Scotch, that Johnny Walker Black—the best—came back and called him in the bathroom and he was playing. I went like that to my coat, so he said—"We're going to stop the set now." So they stopped the set and I met him in the *f*'n bathroom, eh, and he said—"How much is that?" and I said—"Forget about it." So anyway, he opened it up and this ain't a word of a *f*'n lie. He opened up that bottle of *f*'n Scotch and it was a forty-ouncer of Scotch, because that's all they sold at the *f*'n bar because they, anyway, they make more money off it. So anyway, he opened up that bottle of *f*'n Scotch and when he got done drinking it, I swear to *f*, there was only about a half bottle of Scotch left in that *f*'n bottle, in one *f*'n drink! One drink and put it in his pocket and he said—"Do you want any?" I said—"No, I can't drink Scotch." So anyway, we went out and he *f*'n played and we got talking and everything, and we were both staying at the Fisher Hotel. So I got going over every ƒ'n night with my guitar and play with him. So this went on for, oh about a week and a half because he had two weeks there and he was moving on. And I said—"Where are you going in the winter time?" He said—"I don't work in the winter time." I said—"What do you do in the winter time?" He said—"I work in the steel plant in Detroit in the winter time, because it's nice and warm in there."

So anyway, so now I didn't see the guy for thirty years right—thirty ƒ'n years. So I ran into him in Ottawa, right. I smashed the whole front of the truck all to ƒ. Dave, I tell that ƒ'n joke all the time. Anyway, I ran into him in Ottawa, right. It was about ten years ago. So anyway, I went out in the back room and I said—"John Lee, you remember me, Dutch Mason?" I said—"I played with you in Hamilton at the Downstairs Club. I went over and got you a bottle of Scotch one night." He said— "I-I-I never been to Hamilton in my life." That was the ƒ'n thing. I said—"Okay." I didn't know what the ƒ to say, so that was the end of the story.

And he was ƒ'n hard to play with. He just changed chords whenever he felt like it and he just ƒ'n went wherever he went and whatever he had to do, he did it. I just watched him and just changed when he changed. Because like, ƒ, what are you supposed to do?

CHAPTER SIX

Highways Through Quebec

Thursday, November 6

Well, that big eight-wheeler movin' down the track
Means your true lovin' daddy won't be comin' back
Well, I'm movin' on, I'd soon be gone
Well, you fly too high for my little old sky, so I'm movin' on.

"I'm Movin' On," Hank Snow

One of the first things we saw after entering Quebec, just before Notre-Dame-du-Lac, was a billboard for a local radio station which we laughed about for half an hour. "CFVD 95.5 FM."

"Well," AJ said as we passed it. "I guess somebody had to get those call letters. CFVD. What's their slogan: CFVD 95.5 FM, *Home of the Clap?*"

I spent most of my time squeezing my head up over the back of the front seat, trying to stay tuned into the conversation. I felt at times like a kid trying to be part of what their parents are talking about when they drive. We pointed out the amazing fact that in Quebec the Irvings now sell beer and wine in their convenience stores.

"Why can they sell beer in grocery stores here when back home they can't?" asked AJ.

We had fun with the names of hotels and bars all along 185 Nord, signs with names like my favourite: Bar Illusion, which was actually quite real looking, although run down; Motel La Vision, which we joked could be nightmares; Motel Royal-Cabano; Motel Jasper; Motel Marie Blanc; Motel Claude; and a place signed Barn Ferme Boucher. AJ laughed, asking if that meant "shut your barn mouth."

"It's not ferme as in close. It's ferme as in farm."

"St. Louis-de-Ha-Ha is my *f*'n favourite," said AJ. And you've got to admit, it is a funny name. It makes people laugh.

This province is always under *f*'n construction. It doesn't matter where you go or when you go, everything's always ripped to *f*'n shreds.

Dutch was right. We passed through construction and detours all the way to Highway 20, which begins at Rivière-du-Loup. It takes forever at the best of times, let alone late at night.

AJ added: "If I see one more orange and white pylon, I'm going to completely *f*'n lose it."

I said they looked like the hats from *The Cat In The Hat*, wondering if Dutch had ever read Dr. Seuss. I guessed not.

We spent the night in Montmagny at a little place called Motel Wigwam. It's book-ended by the Restaurant Bangkok on one side and by La Maison D'Orient on the other. Surprisingly, this deep into Quebec, there was also an Irving in the vicinity, making us Maritimers feel at home.

I shared a room with Carter. Barry and Charlie bunked together and AJ was with Dutch, because he likes to always be where the action is, which is why he always wants to drive for Dutch. This would be our sleeping arrangement for the entire tour.

AJ, AJ!

Dutch looked at me.

AJ is never *f*'n around when you want him. Dave, would you push me into the room and bring in my *f*'n bag?

Just as I was pushing Dutch's wheelchair to the table so he could have a smoke, AJ came in with Carter and Charlie.

"You're not thinking of staying in Dutch's room are you, Dave?" asked AJ. "You might end up seeing the frog."

When I asked what the hell he was talking about, the guys laughed and changed the subject to food.

It was around two when we'd stopped, which everyone thought would still be good for getting a pizza delivered to the hotel. The desk clerk tried to tell us in badly broken English he doubted we'd get anything that late. But the guys were determined, so we spent half an hour pouring over the yellow pages in Dutch's room, calling places that had always just closed. Dutch, of course, was naked on his bed, chain-smoking Marlboros.

If we hadn't been driving over the *f*'n construction, we'd have been here an hour ago. If we keep running into this much construction, maybe we'll get to *f*'n Toronto by December. Maybe we can play some Christmas parties.

We discussed the merits of Restaurant Bangkok over La Maison D'Orient.

I'm not having ƒ'n Chinese food even if there is one open. I'm just going to sleep.

Four cigarettes later, Dutch did just that—anything to escape our continuing talk about Quebec construction and our astonishment over fact that Irvings sell beer and wine in Quebec.

The rest of us settled on La Maison D'Orient, thinking the premise of Restaurant Bangkok in Montmagny was less plausible.

❖ ❖ ❖ ❖

The next morning, in spite of when we'd gone to bed, we had to be up and in the Motel Wigwam's small dining room by eight o'clock. AJ's late arrival at Dutch's apartment had put us way behind schedule. We had a hell of a time maneuvering Dutch's wheelchair between the tables and the booths. In spite of not having much rest, Dutch was still in a talkative mood.

We got our coffee and each placed an order. Dutch and I were at the end of a table with his wheelchair angled so people, including the waitress, could still get by. She was cute and a bit wary of us, as if we looked like a bunch of musicians. She was polite but didn't really engage in any eye contact. I decided that wouldn't have been the case if we were younger.

"You know, Dutch, if we were in our twenties or thirties, she would have stayed and talked more with us. Funny thing about age, eh? I'll be fifty in a few months. That's friggin' weird when you stop and think about it."

Well, I was born in 1938, February 19, 1938.

I quickly did the math.

"You ever think much about where you came from, about being from Lunenburg and Kentville?"

Well, I lived in Lunenburg until I was eleven years old. I lived there with dad and I had two buddies of mine that I ƒ'n don't know where they are now and as a matter of fact, I played in Lunenburg about, oh, six months ago or something like that and it's going, yeah, it's going.

"I missed that gig. Don't know if I've ever played Lunenburg. What's it like for you going back to play in your hometown and seeing people from your early days?"

I never seen them like, you know, for years and years and so I asked some of the older people down there, the ƒ'n older people down there are ƒ'n probably the same age as me, but I think of them as being older cause they talk old, you know what I mean.

"So does it feel strange when you go back there now? I know sometimes when I go back to Montreal it can feel weird." Another rather pointless attempt at contributing to the conversation. I wanted to add something because it made me feel as though I was truly part of the Dutch circle, *un vrai*, as they say in Quebec.

Whenever this happens, this speaking out of turn or about something seemingly irrelevant, it reminds me that I'm still really a novice. It makes me feel like the character Albert Brooks played in the movie *Lost In America*, where, inspired by his favourite movie, *Easy*

Rider, he tries to rebel against the oppressiveness of the business world by dropping out and heading for the open road—in a Winnebago with a microwave that browns. In one telling scene he gives the thumbs up to a Harley driver who is passing him with Steppenwolf's anthem playing in the background. He feels solidarity with the freedom and rebelliousness of the biker. The feeling is not reciprocated as he gets the finger in return. I must have looked something like that pulling up outside Dutch's place earlier in the day in the Titanium Silver Camry— my Winnebago.

Like I mean it's kind of hard to explain that because like when you're in the business we're in, we're *f*'n twenty years old all our life. You know really I think that's the way you think. But I was talking to women down there that *f*'n went to school with me that lord *f*'n Jesus looked like they dragged them out of a casket, you know what I mean, they look old like *f*'n him.

Dutch was pointing to AJ.

No, but they look old, you know.

AJ, from the other end of the table, couldn't resist. "And you look just like you did in high school, Dutch!"
Dutch asked for the cream and just rolled his eyes.

Anyway, one woman came up to me who knew about one of the kids I used to hang out with—his name was Angus Walters, same as the captain of the *Bluenose,* eh—and the other guy's name was Ronnie and she said that Ronnie was around and Angus was living in British

Columbia. And I often *f*'n wondered about that. I just wondered about what ever happened to him.

The way Dutch tells it, playing music was an integral part of his family life, even as a child.

When I was eleven years old, my father bought a restaurant in Kentville, right, and actually didn't buy a restaurant at first. He went up there to sell, he was selling fish out of a truck, you know, and then he bought a restaurant and yeah, he bought a restaurant after that and then he was playing in a band, Dixieland stuff, eh, you know, so that's how I got started playing. I went to K. C. A. until I was in grade ten and then I got out and I was a major in the army cadets there. All kinds of *f*'n bullshit went on, half of it I can't remember.

I did like Kentville. It was like a sports town and like in our school, it was like an army cadet type of school because the principal of our school was a captain in the real army and I was good at being a soldier or whatever the *f* I was then, and like I was up in the cadets and I actually *f*'n liked it and the principal took me down to the recruiting office to get me in the army so I could have been an officer when I came out. I was already the rank of major in the cadets. But I would have had to go to Chilliwack or some *f*'n place and then I got to thinking—*f* this—I think I'll just play guitar, you know. I didn't want to go in the army.

The thing is I liked the army cadets and I liked everything about it, but I got to thinking, like *f*, I'll be coming out of the army cadets saying I want "that done" right now because, you know, you still have that attitude. But I would never have had that attitude, you know, because I seen guys that came out of the *f*'n army and Jesus, they ran their family like a ƒ'n—like "do this, do that, get this, get that, over here, right now, come here"—and that kind of stuff and I got to thinking, ƒ, I don't want any of that, you know, I just want to go play, you know.

Anyway, that's the way I grew up in Kentville, like that. And if you played baseball and you played hockey, that would get you through school. Being in the army cadets would get you through school. All that shit would get you through school because that's the kind of school it was.

But I was ƒ'n terrible at school. I had no interest whatsoever in any of the subjects. I just ƒ'n hated school. What I liked—being in the army cadets and I liked playing ball, liked playing hockey, you know— is what got me as far as I got in school.

But my childhood sweetheart, Ginny, who I went to school with— four ƒ'n years of sitting in front of me, after three years in school I finally started noticing that she was really nice looking. I went out with her and I got her knocked up on a train trip to Halifax. We used to play Queen Elizabeth High and I was on the hockey team, right, and I knocked her up on a train trip to Halifax and she was fourteen years old. And we got married. We got married and had a son, Charles. He works in Moncton—real nice ƒ'n kid. He's forty-five and runs the park out there, the animal part of the park in Moncton, out by Magnetic Hill. Real good ƒ'n kid, like you know.

But we broke up after about a year because I wanted to go on the road, like playing. She just left me. I don't know how old I was, seventeen maybe or something like that. And she just left and that was the end of that marriage. And then I just said oh ƒ it, I got to go play, so then I just went and starting playing around in dance halls and that because there were no bars, eh, so we were playing at dance halls and all over the place, you know.

Yeah, my dad had a band. He had a Dixieland band and my mother played in another Dixieland band. Because of that I think I still love Dixieland today. I guess they couldn't get along or something in the same band or whatever. My mother played piano, my father played drums, a standup bass, but then once I got old enough that I was playing drums—I was only about fourteen or something like that, or in around fourteen or fifteen or something, however old I was—we had a trio. My father played bass, I played drums, my mother played piano. So we had a trio.

We stayed together, oh, just about four or five months. Like we played like four or five jobs like that because I wanted to get out and play rockabilly music like Elvis Presley, Gene Vincent—whoever the *f* was around and like Jerry Lee Lewis and that. Then I got a group together. I guess it was a *f*'n group, I don't know. Harold Boates was playing drums and I was playing acoustic guitar and I was singing. I couldn't sing a *f*'n lick but I had to sing because like I was probably a little better looking than the rest of them, you know, and I always had a suit on or something, whatever the *f* I was trying to do. Whatever I was trying to do, whatever.

The food arrived at the Motel Wigwam coffee shop. We all kept staring at the cute Quebec waitress. She ignored us again. Everyone started eating except Dutch, who was too busy talking. He loves reminiscing. His eggs got cold.

Anyway, I played acoustic guitar and then so we couldn't play that good so my mother played piano with me like that and my father played standup bass with us until Seig Shepherd came along, so he could play bass and then my mother, she got doing whatever she was doing, like cleaning the house or some *f*'n thing and I got a guy from the bank, Johnny Fraser. He was just a young guy. He was working at the bank. He got playing piano with us. He's living down in Bridgetown now. I think he's retired now. Most of the *f*'n guys I know are retired or dead.

Me and those early boys, we played every Saturday night at the arena in Kentville and we played there for a year before we knew we were supposed to get *f*'n paid. We just played, eh, and one night this guy came in and he said, "What do you guys make for playing here?" and we said, I said—"What do you mean make?" and he said—"what do you make, money, how much money do you make?"—and I said—"I don't know what you mean"—and he said—"Well, you got to get paid" and we went—"What, like paid?"—you know, it was like a hobby for us, you know. So then we realized, *f*, we had to get paid. So I think we were making six bucks a night or something like that, apiece like six dollars a night. That's about what we're *f*'n making now. It hasn't changed.

We didn't *f*'n know. We just played. We only knew three songs, so we played them frontwards, backwards, sideways, just kept playing the three songs over and over. So finally we learned some new songs, you know.

Later on with the Dutch Mason Trio, me and Kenny Clattenburg and Ronnie Miller, when I was playing both piano and guitar, we were making like $420 a week. To tell you how much that was, cigarettes were thirty-three cents a *f*'n pack and now they're like ten dollars. Anything else I didn't know the price of anyway.

Well then the way we started playing, my mother and father broke up when I was about eighteen and so we were playing at my father's dance hall in New Minas, a dance hall and a bowling alley in New Minas, right. This was after he had the restaurant in Kentville. He gave all that up and he had the dance hall and a bowling alley and a restaurant and everything but he didn't get a *f*'n liquor license, right, so that kind of killed him, you know. But we used to play there at dances. But finally he owed so many *f*'n bills, he said—"We'll go out on the road." So we went out on the road with, there was myself, Harold Boates, Johnny Fraser, Seig Shepherd and Bubsy Brown. There was the five of us and we went on the road and just played in dance halls all over Nova Scotia, New Brunswick and P.E.I., you know. It was the late fifties. I was just playing acoustic guitar, you know, like just an acoustic guitar that you see in country bands, and then after a while, I started playing electric guitar. My dad bought me this electric National guitar, you know the steel, shiny ones. It had something like nineteen buttons on it but I just worked the volume control mostly.

I remember Bubsy Brown came in the store one day and he had—I'll never *f*'n forget this—he had on a leather jacket, right, and on the leather jacket had paint down the sleeves like, of this thing, and it had hearts, diamonds, spades and clubs in black and he had his hair all combed back, with long sideburns like that, you know, and he said—"I hear you boys are looking for a guitar player." And then that's how we started the *f*'n band. We had two guitars and drums. And then Seig—Frank Shepherd was his real name—Seig we used to call him—he's dead now, died in Orlando, Florida. I got him there playing electric bass. We had one of the first electric basses around. We used to take old jukeboxes, tear them apart and there was an electrician right next door who used to put in an extra tube for us and then we'd made our own boxes and put the speakers in them, speakers that gave it the extra deepness like that and we had a "Kay" electric bass.

We played rockabilly, like Jerry Lee Lewis stuff and Elvis tunes, Carl Perkins, and that. That's the kind of stuff we played. But I was listening to B. B. King before, in the restaurant my father had in Kentville. The guy who came used to leave extra records for the jukebox, like them old '78 Wurlitzer jukeboxes, like the kind they had on Happy Days, and they would leave extra records for you to put on there, like you know, and I used to change the records and I would put in the *f*'n tunes that I liked, so I had "Sweet Little Angel" and stuff like that on there, you know. Nobody ever *f*'n played it but me, you know, I would be putting the money in to play it like that. But I liked blues right and when I said I wanted to play the *f*'n blues, everybody in the band thought I was *f*'n crazy, you know. But that's what I wanted to play. I wanted to play blues.

I mean I was eighteen or nineteen, something like that. But nobody else wanted to *f*'n play it, like the guys in the band said—"What do you know? It's going to be terrible"—and it was, you know. I tried to play a blues *f*'n song, like we played something like "Sweet Little Angel" and the dance floor just *f*'n cleared. There just wouldn't be nobody there and then you played "Johnny B. Goode" or something, the *f*'n floor would be full. They were right, but I was right too, like you know. Anyway, I thought I was right.

We couldn't play the blues at first cause we couldn't push the strings to make the right sound. Everybody just had these Black Diamond strings and they were all wound strings instead of single thread. So we mixed and matched banjo strings to the guitars so we could learn to push the strings, to bend them to get the blues sound.

Oh, and we had a fifteen-minute radio show every *f*'n Wednesday I think it was or something like that. We were on the radio for fifteen minutes every week and we would take requests—people would call in for requests, like kids you know—and we would play these requests for them, if we knew them.

And my mother and father still played with us because we couldn't *f*'n play anything. We weren't that good, you know. Matter of fact, we were *f*'n terrible. But then after a while we started getting all right you know, and then we started like playing and then that passed and then what did I *f*'n do. I got married to Ginny and then I was still playing music when I was married to Ginny and then I came home one day and she just moved and took Charles with her. Her and Charles just left and I came home and there was nobody *f*'n there.

And then I just said, oh *f* it. I got to go play and so then I just went and started playing around in dance halls and that because there were no bars, eh, so we were playing at dance halls all over the place, you know. And there were different guys coming and going and that stuff is kind of hard to remember because it's so *f*'n long ago.

Looking down the table as Dutch, AJ, Carter, Charlie and Barry interacted, it was suddenly easy to envision previous groups of guys in Dutch's bands, as though I'd been there before. Although Rick Jeffery and those guys lived a lot more precariously, every minute on the edge, there was still something about this moment that made it easier to understand. It had a certain feeling. The moment burst as we got our bills, tipped at the table and paid our bills at the cashier.

❋ ❋ ❋ ❋

We couldn't find an English station on the radio to save our lives. As we joked about saying *"au revoir"* to Montmagny, it suddenly occurred to me where we were and I warned AJ about the fact that this stretch of highway is infamous as Quebec's premiere speed trap.

"Thanks for the warning, Dave," he cracked. *"Merci,"* he added.

With nothing on the radio but Quebec morning talk shows and a crackly, staticky CBC station, I was reminded of something.

"Dutch, I've gotta tell you about this one thing you said on that CBC Atlantic Airwaves interview you did a couple of years ago. In it, you're talking about how you were always out there on the road with the band and then guys in the band starting getting commitments, getting married and stuff like that. At one point, you say how there was only you and a few other guys who had stuck it out and stayed out on the road. So the interviewer asked—'Oh, who besides you, Dutch?' There's this pregnant pause and then you come to a realization, right there on tape, as though it was the first time it actually occurred to you. You said—'well, I guess it was just me.' I remember I was driving when I heard it on the air. I laughed my head off. When you were on the road, didn't you used to do something like three hundred gigs a year?"

Yeah, well for one example, I played Albert's Hall in Toronto. I played Albert's Hall for *f*'n ten years and didn't even know it. You know, not thinking about it, must have been *f*'n near ten years because I was there about two months out of a year, you know, two weeks at a time like that because we opened it. Albert's Hall was a blues bar and we drew bigger than anybody, so that's why we were there starting around 1973.

Albert's Hall had *f*'n everybody, every blues guy you can think of played there, that's who played there. One time we stayed in Toronto for about a year and a half and then one *f*'n day, I just got up out of *f*'n bed—we were living at the Westminster Hotel—and I looked out the *f*'n window and said *f* it. I said—"Let's get out of here, let's go back home" and the guys were all ready in about twenty minutes. Just to get the *f* out of Toronto. Nobody ever liked Toronto. I don't. People in Toronto don't even like Toronto, you know.

Except that Toronto was a place for, like if you're talking about women, women in Toronto actually wanted to pick you up. I mean they'd just come by and grab you, like let's go. I'd say—"I ain't going f'n no where. I'm drinking. Leave me alone." But once in a while, I'd go. I mean obviously, I'm human, you know, I'd go. Like if she was really nice looking or something. In that way, Toronto was a good place.

Another time we went away on the road, Ronnie Miller and me, and we were at the Downstairs Club in Hamilton. We were with John Lee Hooker and all them guys where they used to f'n play and we were just sitting there and there was just me and Ronnie, sitting at this table. You couldn't buy liquor there but everybody had a bottle. I was sitting there drinking and they sang this f'n song and fuck, something just struck me. The tears came right down my f'n face and I'm trying to look away, like that, and I looked over at Ronnie and jeez, there were tears coming down his f'n face. I said—"Ronnie, what do you think?" He said—"Let's go home." I said—"You got the right idea." We went back to the hotel, packed our clothes and headed right back for Nova Scotia. That was it—f'n home-bred boys, eh? Just homesick but jeez, it just put the cap on it, eh. And I forget what the f'n song was, but it was terrible. The same old thing. Went back on the road, went back to Ontario and came back home, went to Ontario, and you know. I just gave up, you know what I mean. But whatever the tune was, it just tore the f'n heart right out of you.

❊ ❊ ❊ ❊

Dutch sounded to me as though he and Ronnie Miller had walked right out of a scene from "Goin' Down The Road," one of the quintessential films of the Maritime experience. It's the story of two unlucky Nova Scotians who decide to head to the big city—Toronto—but who discover that their idyllic paradise is not what they had bargained for.

The movie seems so real at times to the lives of Maritimers, of people rushing off to Southern Ontario in the fifties and sixties. These two beer-drinking party boys rent a tiny apartment, get grunt-work jobs and end up in a new-found life of poverty. There's no sugar-coating this story. My favourite part of the film is two back-to-back scenes where the Nova Scotians are arrested for being drunk somewhere in downtown Toronto. They're told by the police sergeant at the jail that they get to make one phone call between them. In the next sequence, it's morning and the camera crawls as it pans their silent jail cell. You slowly recognize the passed-out bodies of the protagonists, who are surrounded by half-emptied Chinese food takeout containers—they had used their one phone call like true blues men! Maybe that is the reason why I loved the Maritimes at first sight—there is something like the blues about the Maritime experience. There is a certain attitude: common to both is a joyful resignation towards adversity.

❊ ❊ ❊ ❊

None of us had apartments, most of us were just on the road, period. We wouldn't have a ƒ'n place. The road was where you lived. It would go on for a year. You'd just have nowhere to go. I don't even know if I missed having a place to live because I was ƒ'n drunk all the time and I just went through it, you know.

"But you must have been a pretty tight band, playing three hundred gigs a year?"

Yeah, but I mean the band was always just a good ƒ'n band anyway. We played and played and played so much that we just said ƒ it. We'd just wake up and start *f*'n drinking and maybe go downtown and have a sandwich or have something to eat in some place and go in and buy some clothes or some *f*'n thing and come home and fall asleep around six o'clock, wake up at nine and then take a shower, get shaved, put our clothes on and head for the bar and start drinking again. One constant cycle, never *f*'n stopped. We weren't like most people who get up at the same time every day and to go work. Well, good for them. Like seeing people get up in the morning made me happy knowing I didn't have to *f*'n do it. It was a job that I liked. It's hard to find a job that you like. I mean there's probably two hundred meat cutters in Nova Scotia that want to be *f*'n guitar players. But they'll never be guitar players, you know. It's hard to find a job that you like. I mean, isn't that the truth?

I never really had another job besides playing music. I mean I worked in my father's restaurant as a short order cook when I was about *f*'n thirteen or fourteen, just making hot sandwiches and fish and chips and stuff like that, and then I worked for one week at the Cornwallis Inn as a bus boy. Everything else has been music.

I wanted to be a lawyer. I would have been a good *f*'n lawyer. I would have been a good lawyer. Just to *f* up people. No, no, I just thought I'd be a good lawyer. Because I can talk pretty good. Obviously I wouldn't be talking like this, but it just kind of struck me like I'd like to be a lawyer. That's all.

"So having a job as a musician set you apart?"

Dave, when we were first playing, when we were kids like that, we got in a lot of fights because we were in a *f*'n band, right, and the other guys were like hockey players or just guys hanging around like that, you know, so that's how we got in a lot of *f*'n fights too.

We looked different and we dressed different and, you know, it was just a different thing and all the girls *f*'n wanted to go out with us because we were like musicians, you know. In other words, they were saying—"Fuck the hockey players and the baseball players and let's go with the musicians."—Anyway, the girls wanted a little mystery or excitement in their lives, you know.

I didn't even think about it like that. Like I still don't think about it like that. Never thought about it like that. Like you get to see a lot of women and everything but I never thought of it as picking up women. There are guys in bands that just want to play in bands to pick up women. I never thought of it like that. I just figured, *f* it, I'm doing a job, I'm playing. I like to play music, you know, and if a girl happens to come along, that's fine.

There was a wry smile forming on Dutch's face and he paused for a while.

I mean, Dave, how many *f*'n jobs can you get where you get to do exactly what you want to do and get girls coming around and everything. I always just had this idea that I wanted to be a musician and that's exactly what I turned out to be. And I had an idea for *f*'n Garrett to be a musician. I always wanted that in my *f*'n life. I wanted that and it *f*'n happened, so I'm really lucky like that, you know.

I just wanted to play music and make a living.

"You know what I'm going to ask you—now don't laugh, but I've always wondered Dutch—do you have any hobbies or anything like that or has it always been just the music?"

Besides music?

"Yeah, besides the music."

Well, I jerk a lot. Yeah, I jerk a lot.

Dutch laughed.

I think of things and jerk a lot. No, now what the *f* would be my *f*'n hobbies? You know what. I used to, and still do, collect knives. Don't ask me *f*'n why, I'll never know, but I collected knives and watches.

"What about rings? I like rings too and I've heard that you are the guy to buy rings from."

Yeah, I collect rings too, jewelry in particular and knives and *f*'n shit like that. Don't ask me why, I don't know, but I was just always fascinated by *f*'n jewelry and rings and watches and shit.

"What about Cadillacs? Didn't you almost *collect* Cadillacs?"

No, as a matter of fact, this Cadillac here that I got is the first one that I've had for *f*'n years, but I had a lot of them before that. I had every *f*'n thing. Any *f*'n type of car that they had, I had it, you know.
I think maybe my hobby was buying drinks for people. Like I used to travel through the *f*'n people like that and talk to them, buying people *f*'n drinks and that kind of shit and I liked doing it.

"Did you ever think that you would be famous? Some musicians seem to crave the attention."

I had no ideas about going out there and being like Elvis Presley or anything, none of that *f*'n bullshit. You know, I played this place when I was about seventeen or eighteen and we were out back and they had kind of a little dressing room, even though it was in a school, right, and about twenty girls came up and they said—"Shake for us"—and I said—"What?"—like I used to go through them Elvis Presley movements. They just said—"Shake for us"—so I *f*'n made a few moves and they all screamed and yelled. What the *f* is wrong with people when they want that *f*'n shit—"Just shake for us"—didn't give a *f* about the singing, about the playing or nothing. Just—"Shake for us." What a bunch of *f*'n idiots. Just—"Shake for us."

You know what's really *f*'n interesting though, Dave. I'm an introvert doing an extrovert's *f*'n job, you know what I mean. When I'm alone, I want to be *f*'n alone—alone—and when I'm playing, I'm playing, you know. I got like two different personalities like that. I'm an introvert doing an extrovert's job.

Mostly we would play a house job. We would play some places for two *f*'n years. We went into Sullivan's in Halifax for a long time. When we went into Sullivan's, I said—"Boys, drink as much as you can possibly drink" and they said—"Why?" and I said—"Just drink." So everybody drank and then at the end of the week, I said—"Jeez, you scared Sullivan," whose first name was Garrett. He said—"Jesus Christ, you drank more than I'm supposed to pay you. You're going to have to stay another week." Two years later, we were still there. I ended up naming Garrett after him.

We drank so *f*'n much that he just kept holding us over, but the crowds got so ƒ'n big every night of the week that he couldn't lose and neither could we. So that's how we stayed there. So then we went right from there to another ƒ'n place for a year and a half, the Wyse Owl, over in Dartmouth.

This was in the late sixties and seventies. We were at the Wyse Owl for a long time. We almost lost the gig when Jack Jeffery, who played bass for a while, got in a fight over there and tried to stab somebody with a bayonet or something. We had to get him out of the band or we couldn't stay there. He was a hard fish. Jack was a good guy but he had that look in his eye though.

After Jack and the Wyse Owl we went straight to Toronto. I went to Toronto a couple of times before that when I was younger, you know, and I took different bands up there. Different guys, like Ronnie Banks and Garry Blair, Bubsy Brown. Different bands like that and we played around and then we came back home and then we went to Saint John, New Brunswick, and played and then we played in Moncton. We were all over the ƒ'n place. And a lot of the time, we were out of work a lot, sleeping in cars and sleeping in trucks and sleeping at the Halifax Holiday Inn bathroom and stuff like that, you know.

"You don't really think of that when you see the band on stage, about how hard it can be to be on the road."

I remember around that time we were playing in Dartmouth, there was a town drunk there and I used to get along with him really ƒ'n good because I used to feel sorry for him and so I let him stay with me, right. So this ƒ'n night in the wintertime and it was cold, and he said—"Jesus Christ, I know a place to stay." Where he was talking about was an old taxi stand, down underneath the Matador Club, and so anyway, we went down there. It was ƒ'n cold man, no heat down there, nothing. So I laid on the floor and—I don't know how I did it—but I fell asleep. When I woke up in the morning, I tried to get up and I couldn't ƒ'n move. The pipes broke and the water came out all over the floor along and my hair was stuck to the floor, frozen to the floor along with my clothes. I was frozen to the ƒ'n floor. I had to get the guy to run out and get hot water and dump it on my head so that I could ƒ'n pull myself up.

That's the kind of ƒ'n places we used to be, those are the things we used to do, eh. But I liked that ƒ'n guy. He was a good old ƒ'n guy. He used to get on the ferry in the night time and he'd just go back and forth until they said he had to get off because the ferry stopped running. He stayed on the ferry because it was warm. One time, they went to wake him up and he didn't wake up. He was dead. He died right on the ƒ'n ferry. I liked him. He was a real, nice ƒ'n old guy. Yeah ƒ, what a ƒ'n sin. What a ƒ'n sin.

"I remember seeing you play or even playing with you and seeing so many people coming up and always wanting to talk to you, and you talked to everybody."

I don't mind talking to them if they just stay away from me. But now—it's the wheelchair. Back on the road before, I always just went out and went through the crowd, talked to everybody. Especially when I was walking I would talk to everybody. It makes me more personal for you, like you know, and people are saying—"Jeez, not stuck up or anything, he's a normal fuckin' guy"—and that's how people, I guess, think, you know.

"I certainly noticed that Ricky was kind of nervous and shy and insecure whenever you'd talk to him privately. But then he would come out on stage and be this outrageous kind of guy who looked like a cross between a hit man and a peacock, all dressed up."

Dave, I was never insecure about any *f*'n thing. As for Ricky, well, that's what made his nerves so *f*'n bad. But for me, I mean I was never *f*'n shy or nervous about anything like that. I always talked to everybody. Or at least I did until I got in this *f*'n wheelchair. Now when people get too close to me and they're stepping on me and then bang, crash, but they're just trying to be nice.

AJ was fixated on the highway, and the forward movement of the lumbering Cadillac was making Dutch sleepy. Part of me also wanted to sleep, but another part wanted to imagine the gigs and the venues. Dutch seemed happy to be back on the road, as were the rest of the guys. The road is where blues men and women live, moving along the margins of a society they can never truly be part of, or even the underclass whose voice they try to represent. They cannot exist within the society or outside of it, which is why Jimi Hendrix had to die. Like Janis Joplin, he could not live within the norms of the community and could only survive for so long on the edge. He had nowhere to go but out.

Living on the margins may make for a hard life but it gives the blues musician a different and perhaps truer viewpoint about real life—work, sex, death, alcohol, drugs, success, failure—than we who live at the centre of things. They have no real, established stake in the dominant order so nothing can prevent them from speaking that truth. They have nothing to lose. Dutch suffers for his choices in life, but he's done exactly what he wanted and said exactly what he wanted to say.

Meanwhile, I was pre-occupied with the tour, although waiting for the gigs to start also made me feel like a kid on Christmas Eve. And the gift, for me, was the first place we played: Grossman's Tavern in Toronto. The difference was that I sensed the novelty would not wear off. Playing with Dutch is always something to look forward to, all the more so in venues and in cities where I'd never played.

❈ ❈ ❈ ❈

Somewhere around Chatham, the 401 outbound Toronto traffic had built up to its norm for that time of day. Thankfully we were going against the gridlock and heading into the city. We hadn't seen Carter's van for half an hour, but we reassured ourselves they weren't far behind. We ended up in a debate about how quickly a car can stop when it's traveling at 120 or 130 kilometers per hour. The highway signs warn drivers to keep at least two chevrons between cars in case someone is breaking up ahead. AJ was hanging one chevron behind the cars and trucks in front of us, which certainly made me nervous. I'd been trying to read in the backseat when this chevron thing came up.

"Aaaaiiii Jaaayyy, I'm trying to read back here but you're scaring the shit out of me by driving so close."

AJ ignored me.

I'm scared to ask what you're *f*'n reading Dave. And how can you read in the *f*'n car, anyway?

I had been talking to Dutch's former wife Pam one time about what books I was reading. I was working on the *Bacchae*, the play by Euripides. She told me that she was always reading something. I asked her what Dutch liked to read.

59

"The joke between us was that they used to always have on Much Music these little interviews with musicians, and one of the guys used to ask their guests, 'What's your favourite book?' So I always asked that to Dutch—Dutch only read about five books in all the time I've known him. I don't even think it was five. Because I read all the time, I said 'why don't you read?' So I said—'Here's what you'll say if you are ever asked this question'—he should say he reads the classifieds in the newspaper and the auto trader. That would be his big thing in life to read. But he did read a book, I can't remember what it was. Oh and he used to read the book of lists.

"I used to read to him. Virginia, one of his old girlfriends, gave him this big thick book of lists, and I used to read it to him at night. He would say, 'read to me,' and I would. That's when we lived at Brunswick Towers. He's just not a reader; Garrett is the same way. And I can't sleep without reading; I'm the opposite.

"His hobby used to be the Buy/Sell/Trade. Everybody in Halifax used to say if they needed stereo equipment—and we lived in Truro the whole time—'call Dutch.' We used to have cars right, left and centre in the driveway. He'd buy a car, fix it up, sell it, but never make a profit. I mean he'd sell it when we needed the money or something like that, but he'd lose money every time. I think there was one car we might have made a profit on. But we used to go to yard sales all the time, even when we used to drive up to the Valley and Garrett would be in the back seat. All of a sudden there would be a yard sale sign and Garrett and I would go—'Oh, no, let's just go to Nanny's. Let's get to where we're going'—but he would stop and look at the yard sales.

"We used to go up where Ronnie Banks and Bertha were. We'd wake up Saturday morning, and Dutch and Bertha would drive all around the Valley to the yard sales. I didn't want to go. I said — 'No, I'll stay here with Ronnie, you guys just go,' and that was their thing. Dutch would say—'Come on Bertha, you got to go to bed early. We got to get up and go to the yard sales'—that was his big treat."

Those thoughts from Pam reminded me further of the divide between Dutch and me. Hardcover volumes of Greek philosophy versus Buy/Sell/Trade. It reminded me of the contrast he drew one time between one set of highbrow, esoteric lyrics and what he thought regular people understood. It was a Beatles's lyric, "I Am The Walrus," I think it was, and he compared it to the Chuck Berry tune "No Particular Place To Go." It doesn't matter what the rest of the conversation was about—we were probably talking about songs and artists that we liked or that he knew. What mattered was Dutch's attitude:

I mean a song goes—"I am he, since you are he, since you are I"—now what the *f* is that? I'll take what Chuck Berry said in that song—"Ridin' along in my automobile, my baby beside me at the wheel." I mean at least he's *f*'n saying something, like something real, like that, do you know what I mean?

There are still times when I pick up a book on Plato and I think back to Dutch's point of view.

AJ finally agreed to slow down a bit and I was able to relax and read as we passed by Chatham, Pickering and wheeled our way on the 401 to the Yonge Street exit for downtown Toronto.

CHAPTER SEVEN

Toronto

Friday, November 7

Two bit hand at 21, that's all I ever get,
Blackjack hand mister dealer man, you'd better pay off this last bet
Go Down Gamblin', say when you're running low
Go Down Gamblin', you may never have to go.

"Go Down Gamblin'," David Clayton Thomas/F. Lipsins

Toronto the good, Toronto the bad. Everybody in Canada has an attitude and a feeling about the city. But no matter how people feel about it, they always end up coming back here for something or other. Living now in the Maritimes, I wonder every time I go to Toronto why it is that the closer you get to the centre of the universe, the worse it smells.

Grossman's Tavern is on Spadina, at the corner of Cecil Street. Heavy traffic, Toronto street cars and throngs of people add to the daily bustle of Chinatown. It all dissolves at dusk into bits of garbage—mostly paper—blowing into little tornadoes on street corners, and the city starts to feel vacant and lonely. When it does, Grossman's becomes the perfect place to duck into: the half-filled pitchers of beer, the smoky haze and the anticipation of hard-driving blues. They say that a good bar is like "a cathedral of thought." If that's so, then Grossman's must be the St. Peter's of Toronto. The tavern was opened in 1948 by the Grossman family and was sold to the Louie family in the mid 1970s. The place is a legend in its own right, having become Toronto's unofficial home of the blues. The Cecil Street side of the building's thirty-foot-high aluminum-clad exterior is covered in red and green murals of blues performers against a backdrop of greenish-black paint. The front, on Spadina, is "you-can't-miss-it" pink with more murals in bright yellow. Inscribed at the bottom of the wall is a credit to the creative energy of the "Cecil (St.) and Harbourfront Community Centres Graffiti Transformation Project—1999." Totally out of place and mounted at the centre of the elaborate mural on the Spadina side of the building is a HomeLife Realty sign, the office for which is on the second floor. The Louies, it turns out, are, amongst other things, into real estate.

Next door is a small storefront housing a peep show, which we all joked we would visit after we finished loading in our gear. The entire neighbourhood was alive with food and retail. Immediately opposite on Spadina was the "Sun-lit Trading Company," the "OK Brother Trading Company," "Vogue Spot Inc. Retail/Wholesale," and a place called "Quality Watches and Happy Toys." We decided we were definitely going shopping at any place selling *happy toys*.

Everybody and their grandmother of note has played Grossman's: The Downchild Blues Band, Jeff Healey, Kid Bastien and the Happy Pals, Burton Cummings, Robert Priest, Philip Sayce, Holly Cole, Blue Rodeo, Jane Siberry, Sam Moon, Alannah Myles, Amanda Marshall, Danny Marks, Colin James and, of course, Dutch.

You can get an all-day breakfast like steak'n eggs or "The Famous Grossman's Burger," off the menu, but the attraction is not the food. It's got more to do with the weathered feeling of the place, that blues bar sensibility made real by the layers of grime and ashes. "Not a case of bad housekeeping," as writer Alex Lukashievsky once penned, "but of character. This is the real deal."

Because it is first and foremost a blues bar, Grossman's is supposed to be decrepit. Because it is a blues bar icon, it is especially so. The linoleum floor looks like the original, and a large, roughly-trimmed hunk of broadloom covers the corner where the bands set up. It is as smoke-stained and as dark as the blackest film noir. Particularly memorable is Grossman's south wall. It's covered in sepia-toned wallpaper of naked women who are mostly obscured by a rogue's gallery of performers who've played the bar, a substantial collection of 8" by 10" black-and-white glossies that cover most of the bar's interior.

The place is famous for having Toronto's longest-running Sunday night jam—eighteen years from the day the government of Ontario made Sunday drinking legal. The Sunday event means there's live music seven days a week all year long.

The thirty-five-foot bar is sparse and dark. When we first arrived around six in the evening, there wasn't a soul in the place except an or-dinarily-dressed bartender bargaining rent with a guy in his mid-twenties who was obviously a new tenant in one of the Louie apartment buildings. The bartender I found out later was Tony Louie, one of the sons. The tenant seemed to want the apartment, wherever it was, nearly for free, including a new fridge. He pleaded his case on behalf of his infant son and his wife, who he kept saying was half Chinese. Tony was firm regarding his position and was not prepared to yield. I'd want him on my negotiating team.

❈ ❈ ❈ ❈

We rushed to check into the Bond Place Hotel at Dundas and Bond streets in downtown Toronto, between Yonge and Church. The deal they offered took us off guard. You paid a Toonie for the first night and $115 per room for the second night. Of course, you had to stay the second night to get the Toonie deal. So each room ran us about fifty-eight dollars plus tax. It was the strangest hotel deal I'd ever heard of, but the place was incredibly central, the rooms were okay and they had pretty good access for Dutch's wheelchair. The bar in the lobby was called Monika's and Dutch wanted to know if she was in.

"It's just a name, Dutch," I said. "It's just a name."

I *f*'n know that Dave. I *f*'n know that.

That night before the gig, with everything set and the perfunctory sound check out of the way, Carter and a couple of the guys took a stroll to check out the store windows as most of the shops were closed or closing. Dutch and AJ were still back at the hotel. I asked a petite woman behind the bar for a dark rum and coke. I just wanted to get the feel of the place. She looked to be in her late thirties and turned out to be one of the owners. Amy Louie is one of six siblings, which include two eye doctors, a teacher and two realtors, all of whom still work shifts during the week. She was gregarious and thrilled to have Dutchie back at her family's famous bar.

"He has such a style," she says. "He's a great entertainer. He just attracts your attention."

It had been a few years since Dutch played Grossman's, but the effect had obviously been indelible.

"I think he's popular because he has a passion for what he does. Some guys get up there and their level of enthusiasm just doesn't match the lyrics. Dutch rallies the audience. He makes them emotionally charged.

"I've been in here and heard so many acts, even good acts, where you'll be talking with someone and the music is just like white noise. And I'm here a lot so I don't pay as much attention. I even remember once Burton Cummings playing here and it was like the white noise just kept on. But when Dutch plays, it breaks through. Even I stop and listen.

"Plus he's such a cuddly-looking guy."

I couldn't wait to tease Dutch about that line. But Amy should know about quality entertainment. This is where the country's greatest acts have played and where Jeff Healey was discovered at the age of fourteen. Then she said something right out of the blue, right from her heart, that really stuck with me.

"He should have been more famous than he is."

I've heard that said about Dutch before, especially about his great band of the seventies and eighties. All the blues names knew and respected him and he was phenomenally popular in Canada. However, he never really tried to break into the American market. Next to our reputation for being polite to a fault, it is one of the great Canadian clichés that we fail to acknowledge success unless you've made your mark in the States. In the case of the blues, however, this ideal is not misplaced.

Dutch never went because he never planned his career. He never planned much of anything, but especially not his career. He just played music. The story goes that the "music business" is more business than music, but that was never true for Dutch. It was all music for him. Although it is a regional stereotype, Maritimers do seem to prefer their home, their place, to money and success. It always strikes me when I meet someone with greatness that they love what they do with an almost blind singleness of purpose. They do it because it impels them the way hunger or fatigue impels us all. For Dutch, that love was playing music, so he never gave the States or fame much of a thought.

Amy went on from the subject of Dutch to explain that Grossman's actually runs itself.

"There is no manager," she says. "We all have our little jobs."

Her *little job* includes booking all the entertainment—seven days a week—running the web site, taking her turn at running the bar and being the friendly enforcer.

"I grew up here, so I don't really drink. I've been hanging out here since I was sixteen or seventeen."

I discovered from Amy that the Louie family are technically the Lui family; when patriarch "Sam," now in his mid-seventies, arrived from China in 1955, they misspelled his name at immigration, and it stuck. Sam and his wife, referred to by a select few as Mamma Louie, are on the premises at ten o'clock or ten-thirty every morning and, except for a brief break in the afternoon, are usually there until three or four o'clock in the morning. Mrs. Louie has been saying the same thing for the entire thirty years they've owned and operated the bar: "The music's too loud," which of course nobody can ever do anything about.

Amy has a philosophy these days about booking bands, always a complex matter given the nature of musicians.

"If you don't have e-mail, you can't get booked here anymore."

That e-mail pre-requisite made me wonder how we ever got the gig. The booking never happened through my e-mail system, so who could it have come through? Or did we get the gig because Dutch still owed them a bar tab from so long ago? Probably not, but you never know.

Amy added that bands destined for Grossman's virtually never cancel, mostly because it's become an honour to play there.

Things have changed in recent years, partly she says, as a result of drinking and smoking laws. I mentioned how worried the bands are back home about the new smoking by-laws. Bands like Dutch's used to play the entire week, but now only do single nighters or Friday/Saturday gigs. The late Saturday afternoon show featuring Dixieland Jazz, from four to eight o'clock, and the Sunday afternoon jams are huge traditions in Toronto. Bands, especially drummers, hate the Dixieland stuff on Saturday, because the Friday night act has to strike its gear to make way for the regular house jazz band, then quickly reset things when they wind up around nine o'clock Saturday night.

As a bouncer, Amy isn't really afraid of anyone, although she's only about five feet tall.

"Every tough guy has a soft spot," she says, referring even to members of the bike gangs who've frequented the place over the years. She has a line that works its charm on even the most brutal-looking guys, one that brings a smile to their face. If they're acting over the top from liquor or dope or a combination of the two, she has a technique that she first tried on a fellow who prided himself on being the toughest around. Amy remembers him mostly because of a t-shirt he wore, an image of Daffy Duck stretched across his belly. The fatter he got, the bigger Daffy got. The technique that disarmed him, and has worked on others ever since, is this: she cups her hand around her ear and whispers, "I hear your pillow calling you," as though she's talking to a little boy up past his bedtime. She says it always makes people laugh.

Just as Amy finished her story, three lads walked in who looked like they could turn the place on its ear. I decided to finish up my rum and coke and split, but she greeted and talked to them as though they were just regular guys. In the context of Grossman's, I guess they were.

In front of the entire band, I told Dutch before we played that night that Amy Louie thought he was a cuddly guy.

"Careful there Dave," said AJ. "You don't want to cuddle up to Dutch on a long road trip."

We had a great gig. There was no white noise coming from us, only the attention of a packed house both nights. And as Amy predicted, it pissed AJ off to have to strike his drum set Friday night—and reset before the next night's gig—to make way for the Saturday afternoon Dixieland jazz.

On Saturday night we played through the year's third lunar eclipse. We started our first set shortly after ten o'clock. Even from the stage, we could tell that patrons who came in for the next hour or so were talking about the moon and the sun. During our first break, we were all keen to step outside and see what was left of the event, everyone except Dutch.

It's a *f*'n eclipse for jeez sake. A *f*'n lunar eclipse.

I had told Dutch about how Amy Louie gets rid of customers who get out of hand. Close to the end of the night, I noticed her doing exactly what she'd described. Five-foot Amy was at the end of the bar talking to this six-foot-something guy who was obviously completely hammered. He looked like bad news. Between songs, I leaned over to Dutch and prompted him to watch. Just as I did, she cupped her left hand to the back of her ear, leaned in and said something to him. It had to be— "I hear your pillow calling you."

Jeez, look at that. She's *f*'n doing it, just like you said, Dave.

The guy got up laughing, downed the rest of his beer, turned and walked out of the bar. We couldn't believe it.

CHAPTER EIGHT

Ottawa

Monday, November 10

I don't need nobody to tell me 'bout my baby
Because I know she's been doin' me wrong
The word is out, it's all over town
I don't know how anything can take you so long.

"It's All Wrong," Dutch Mason

We were back on the 401 just outside of Toronto, arguing over AJ's driving. AJ can be fidgety at the best of times, which makes me even more nervous. Dutch just doesn't seem to give a shit. We were headed for Ottawa. We passed a sign indicating our destination and AJ joked that he couldn't wait to see Chrètien.

"He's only got a few weeks left in there, a few days maybe even," I said to AJ. "Chrètien is really dragging it out."

I got no response as neither AJ nor Dutch care much about politics or political science. I wanted to talk about it because I was getting tired of talking about bars, hotel rooms, TV, and sex. But there were no takers.

"I doubt we'll see either him or Martin at the Rainbow Room. They just don't strike me as Rainbow Room guys."

Dave, I'm in my late sixties. I might even be the same age as Chrètien. Wouldn't it be funny if we had the same *f*'n birthday.

When Dutch had his sixtieth birthday party at the Halifax Metro Centre, he got a birthday card "from one prime minister to another." I remember laughing when I read it. Chrètien went up in my estimation. I didn't realize that he had such a sense of humour.

Somehow the conversation came up about Barrie, Ontario, because they've got a good jazz and blues festival there. I mentioned that that's where the Canadian Jazz and Blues Hall of Fame is supposed to be. AJ piped up that neither Dutch nor any of the guys in the band had ever been there.

"Jesus Dutch, is that true?" I asked. "You've never been to the Canadian Jazz and Blues Hall of Fame? Even though you were one of the original inductees, with the likes of Moe Kauffman and Oscar Peterson?"

"We should go there," said AJ. "We should *f*'n just go there today!"

I don't know where it is. But here's the *f*'n thing of it. It's like I don't even look at stuff like that. It's just another *f*'n award, you know. I've got a JUNO I use as a doorstop. Because there's people that won awards that I looked at and thought—"That guy deserves that award about as much as I deserve being a *f*'n nuclear physicist," you know what I mean. So it doesn't mean *f*'n that much to me. There are a lot of *f*'n other people they could have taken and put in the *f*'n thing besides me. A lot, a lot of other *f*'n people. So that's why it doesn't *f*'n really bother me.

"But who else do you think is at the same sort of level as you in the blues scene in Canada?" I asked him, as though I wasn't speaking directly to him.

Who could have won that award? All kinds of ƒ'n people. I don't even know, but plenty of them. You know. It's just that you get, I don't know, people get something in their head and they think—"Oh fuck, this guy is whatever and you're not, you're just another fuckin' human being," you know. If they like you as a person, then you're a good guy, you know what I mean, and that's what you should ƒ'n be. But if they don't like you, you'll never get in the ƒ'n hall of fame. You just won't get in. Hall of whatever. Like the Saturday Night Blues award, I didn't even know I won the ƒ'n thing. Fish [Gregg Fancy] told me I won it.

The Saturday Night Blues ƒ'n thing is a big Plexiglas plaque with the Saturday Night Blues logo, the CBC logo. I was the first one in and it's controlled by people that write in and call in, so the public puts you in there, you know what I mean. So if the public likes you as a person, and that's how you get in there, you know what I mean. So I mean like I was the first one in anyway. Fish told me about it, saying—"You won that ƒ'n thing." I said—"What thing?" And he said—"The Saturday Night Blues award." I said—"Fuck, I didn't win any Saturday Night Blues award. What are you talking about?" And he told me about it and I said—"Well, maybe I did win it," and I did.

"Well then what about the one they named after you at the Fredericton Harvest Jazz and Blues Festival, the Dutch Mason Award?"

Yeah, that's kind of a good one, because I mean when you have an award named after you, it's a little ƒ'n different.

"Ricky won that, right?"

Yeah, I was the one that gave it to him.

"I think he was really moved by it. He has the plaque on the wall of his room and he's really proud of it."

Yeah, Ricky thinks a lot. He's a good thinker. He thought a lot about things like that. Me, I never thought about anything in my *f*'n life, you know.

We came to the sign on the 401 for the upcoming exit to Barrie.

"Dutch," piped up AJ. "We need to go to Barrie to see the Hall of Fame. It says it's only 120 clicks."

I don't want to drive three or four *f*'n hours out of our way to see a plaque with my *f*'n name on it.

❖ ❖ ❖ ❖

Carter following in the van didn't know what the hell we were doing when we took the Barrie exit. We had to stop on the side of the highway for AJ to explain he'd gotten his way and talked Dutch into going. I could see the resignation on Carter's face as he passed the back window of the Caddy on the way back to the truck.

Once in Barrie, we asked around about the Hall of Fame, at two gas stations, a taxi driver we flagged down, and two or three people on the street. We were growing skeptical. Dutch was beside himself in the face of AJ's reassurances we'd find the place.

"There's a second-hand CD store," I said. "Let me go in there."

One side of the store window was full of old blues album covers facing out toward the street. The guy inside, a fifty-ish man who looked like he'd know about the blues scene, laughed when I told him he were looking for the Canadian Jazz and Blues Hall of Fame.

"Well, it's supposed to be in Barrie," he said "So is the new performing arts centre it's supposed to be housed in." He was shaking his head, peering over my shoulder to get a glimpse of Dutch parked out front in the Caddy. "So that's really Dutch Mason?"

"That's Dutch," I said, "here to see himself in the Hall of Fame."

"Well, in spite of the guy's best efforts—the guy who was heading up the project—nothing's happened, not yet anyway."

"You mean they announced the inductees," I asked, "they announced the Hall of Fame, but there's no such thing or place?"

"No such thing or place," he confirmed, still shaking his head. "But it will be great for Barrie to have it if it ever does come together."

No more wild *f*'n goose chases AJ! Stay on the *f*'n highway. Let's just get to Ottawa.

❖ ❖ ❖ ❖

Eventually, the conversation returned to normal. We were talking about Ricky's amazing harp playing and about how he had helped me get better as a harp player.

With AJ looking on, Dutch decided to give me the facts, the truth about what he thought when he first heard me play. I had met Dutch through AJ and he always encouraged me and kept asking Dutch to let me get up and play. Ricky would let me use his amp and would give me pointers about how to play with the band. That was back in '94 and '95.

I'm a pretty honest guy, Dave, and I'll tell you exactly the *f*'n way I felt. When I first heard you play harp, I said to *f*'n AJ—"He'll never *f*'n

make it." I said—"He's not going to make it." And then about a year and a half went by and it was like night and day. I said—"The *f*'n guy sounds great"—and then it went on after that and now you can play. But I mean I wouldn't lie about something like that. But that's exactly what I said to AJ—"I don't think he's going to *f*'n make it." And now I'm telling you all this.

Anyway, you do sound good. I don't know a lot about the *f*'n harp, but I know what sounds right and what doesn't sound right. Like Joe Murphy is a good *f*'n harp player. I like Joe's playing. Yeah, I really like Joe's playing. Joe plays more the old style harp, like you know. Whatever the new style is, I don't know.

It's like what I always looked for in players, not just harp, but everyone. I looked for guys who played with simplicity, who were loyal and all that, but who played with simplicity. Like guys who didn't *f*'n try to say everything in one song or just one solo.

❈ ❈ ❈ ❈

I started playing the blues late in life, not much more than a decade ago and I'm forty-nine now. Unlike Dutch and all of the band members who knew at an early age that they were going to devote their lives to the music, I was in my thirties and my commitment was always tempered and partial. I'd already finished my doctorate in political science and had just completed a year working for the Ontario government. My only child, Riiko, was born and Sue and I decided that Sue would return to her medical practice and I would be a stay-at-home dad. In between feedings and diaper changes I took up the harp.

Like a lot of us, I was never confident that the life's work I'd evolved into was really all there was. When I started teaching myself to play the harmonica I could feel the spell the blues casts over people. I felt the music pulling me from my normal centre of gravity. My background is typical, if not more privileged than most. Like me, my father was a university professor in Montreal. I grew up in Westmount and attended private school. On the surface, it appears that I've done what I was designed to do, living out the life charted for someone of my upbringing. Like many, though, the outward conformity of our behaviour masks a distaste for the conventions and constraints of what my mother called proper society.

When I heard the blues for the first time, I got hooked on its sound and feeling and groove. I had borrowed the self-titled record by Taj Mahal. The opening tune is "Leaving Trunk," which begins with a harmonica solo. Embarrassingly, I had to ask a friend what instrument was being played to make that sound, listening to it over and over. I fell in love with the blues and the harmonica. I took a few lessons while still living in Montreal from Dan Robichaud, with whom I became friends and who, like me, would end up in Fredericton. That was in 1991. After ten weeks of lessons, Dan offered me a chance to sit in with his band, an offer I refused—I was too self-conscious. I knew even then that playing in front of a blues crowd is especially daunting because they really know their music well. Dan was aware of how much I wanted to get up and play, and he had no sympathy for my case of nerves.

"You are pathetic, really pathetic," he said.

That stung coming from someone as nice as Dan. But he was right and I promised myself then and there that I'd never again turn down a chance to play, no matter how painful or how excruciating the experience.

My chance at redemption came two years later.

I was living in Fredericton and was at The Dock, a bar that's now defunct, listening to Theresa Malenfant. She was and remains the queen of the blues in Eastern Canada. I knew a friend of her drummer—AJ—who asked her if I could sit in for a number or two. Theresa agreed and, when I got to the stage, leaned over to whisper something in my ear. I fully expected that she would offer words of encouragement for the rookie.

Instead, she said, "You fuckin' better be able to play that thing."

Such was my horrifying introduction to professional stage work. But, Theresa has since become one of my best friends and we have joked about that first meeting. It was through Theresa and AJ, who has also been Dutch's drummer for twenty years, that I got the chance to meet Dutch and the guys in his band. AJ sort of took me under his wing and toured me through the world of the blues players in the Maritimes. AJ is one of the best shuffle drummers in Canada. He has played with just about every blues player in the country and despite numerous offers from other bands, he has always stayed close to home and to Dutch. Like many Maritime musicians, playing with Dutch Mason is what he is most proud of. It gives him a status and a feeling of validation that no other musical or professional accomplishment can match. And so he remains in the Maritimes.

❋ ❋ ❋ ❋

After recounting my often-repeated story about my first time playing with Theresa, AJ and Dutch began competing for the telling of a story in which they were both implicated.

"Theresa and I had our falling outs," said AJ. "She fired me three times and I quit twice, I think it was, but we had a good time together. It's a love/hate relationship. But I'll never forget the time we were playing in one bar and we went on break and I came down to jam with Dutchie because he had to use this awful band out of Saint John. It was bad, and Dutchie had said—"If you ever get a chance during a break, come down and help me out and get up and I'll f'n play with you." So I said—"Okay"—so we got on break with Theresa, but little did I know the club owner decided he was not having a good crowd with Theresa, so he brought her right back on again in ten minutes. I thought I had a half hour break. He wanted to close the bar down at one instead of two and just hold the people. In the meantime, I had run down to jam with Dutchie. We're out there playing—I'm there for one song—and all of a sudden Theresa is standing at the stage and with the bar packed, with Dutchie there playing, and she's standing there with her fist on the stage going—"You're my drummer! You get the fuck out!" Dutchie is going—"The bulldog is coming to get you now, AJ." I said—"Here she comes, holy fuck!" She was wild. Then Dutchie goes—"Oh Theresa, please don't hurt little AJ," right over the microphone.

Like so many others, Theresa also got her start sitting in with Dutch. She was seventeen and the only blues song she knew was "Turtle Blues" by Janis Joplin. To this day, every time she sings that song, she tells the story of her first time on the stage and never forgets to thank Dutch for helping her start her career.

❋ ❋ ❋ ❋

The harp, or harmonica—"lickin' stick" is what Dutch always called it when he introduced Rick—is my constant companion. I mostly play diatonic harmonicas. Each one is in a different key, so I bring twenty-four of them to every gig, one for each key and one extra to be on the safe side. Harps break rather easily. Players tend to use Hohner harmonicas. They are good and the easiest to find. Most harp guys are very particular about the kind they use. Like a lot of players, I use

Special 20's. Some of the older guys, like James Cotton, use Marine Band. They sound great but they're made in part with wood which swells up when they are played hard and the wood hurts my mouth.

To me the harp is more than an instrument; it is the sweet, alluring siren, the temptress within the blues. Dutch used that word one time; he said that the blues was like a "siren wooing" him.

Rick Jeffery would use pretty much whatever he could get his mouth around, even though he used Special 20 a lot too. During the 1994 Fredericton Harvest Jazz and Blues Festival, the year they named the award after Dutch Mason, Rick came to me to borrow an E-Flat harp. He used to play F whenever Dutch sang slow blues, but Dutch's voice had gotten lower over the years and he now needed to use an E-Flat harp. After the song he offered to return it, but Rick being, well, not a healthy man at the best of times, I said: "That's okay Ricky, you keep it." I was happy to give it to him, and besides I didn't want to wrap my mouth around that instrument again. You cannot swap harps like you do guitars!

Of course the harp is only part of what makes the sound. There's also the amplifier. A popular favourite, one of many I've collected, is a Fender Super Reverb made in 1973. Blues guys call it simply a '73 Super Reverb and everyone knows what they're talking about. It's the model Muddy Waters always used. It's what I normally use for gigs and what I take on the road because it sounds good and is the toughest amp ever. I also own a '65 Blackface Vibrolux, a '49 Gibson GA-30 and a '65 Blackface Fender Bandmaster. Musicians are always on the hunt for better and more gear. When they're not talking about it, they're reading magazines about it or looking in used music stores.

With most things *newer* is usually thought to mean *better*. This is not always true though, especially so in the blues world where age and tradition are respected. Blues respects its roots and reveres its elders. Even the gear is personified in this way. Vintage amps are better than new ones. They certainly cost a lot more. Blues players always want to reproduce the sound of the old recordings: the echo of Little Walter's harmonica; the jazzy chords of T-Bone Walker; the sharp, biting, high notes of Albert King. You need the amps and guitars of the fifties and sixties to sound like that. The really great players have all studied the past. They have learned the older styles, the licks and tones of their forefathers. You have to have your own sound, but blues players and fans are purists. You also have to know how the original sounded and even if you play a tune your own way, you have to be respectful of those who played it before you.

✻ ✻ ✻ ✻

I asked Dutch if he'd ever played harp.

No, I played guitar, drums, bass and piano. Guitar was the thing that I liked, you know. I like *f*'n around on the piano. If they had those transposers on the piano now, I'd be able to see where you can put a C and a G, like that, *f*, I'd probably be a fantastic piano player, you know what I mean. Because they have the transposers right on the *f*'n thing.

"Tell Dave how we met Dutch," AJ said. Since playing with Dutch is the most important thing in his life, AJ loves hearing and participating in this story.

Jeez, it was more than twenty years ago if you can *f*'n believe it. I said to Terry Edmonds—I said—"Terry, I got to get a *f*'n drummer, a good *f*'n drummer" and Terry said—"There's a drummer I think might be able to play a shuffle, but he's playing with a rock band." I said—"Well, I don't give a *f* who he's playing with, as long as he can play a *f*'n shuffle. Some kind of shuffle, like that, because a lot of our tunes are shuffles, you know."

So AJ showed up. Fuck, he walked in and he had on a pair of, I think, leather pants or something and some kind of thing and eye makeup. I kept looking at him, thinking like—"What the *f* has he got there." I didn't give a *f* but Terry told me if he's got eye makeup on, he's a fruit. I said—"What?" I said—"How can the man be a fruit. He's just got eye makeup on. Who cares?"

I said—"AJ, here, let's play this *f*'n tune." So we started playing and I said—"AJ, here, I just want to show you something and it will help you out." And I sat down and I showed him, like the left hand, the right hand thing, like that, on the drums. He picked it right up and that was *f*'n it and away we went. And AJ wasn't even gay!

"No, I wasn't even gay," says AJ. "We did about six or seven songs I think it was, and you know, a couple slow ones, a couple of shuffles and then I said—'Well, is that the end of the thing? So what's the verdict?'

"I was playing at the time with a rock band. Anyway, that was back in the eighties, so that's why all that makeup and everything. So anyway, I said—'So what's the verdict?' He said, 'Well we got a job this weekend, so if you want, we're going to go down there and do it.' I think we were doing Windsor and Digby. We had a couple of things all lined up and Dutchie said—'We'll go and try it. I'll give you a month and see what happens because we're going out west in a month.' He said—'If it works out over the next few weeks, then you're in the band.' End of story—twenty years later.

"There was one time when Garry Blair, Dutch's old drummer, who was playing with Frank McKay I think then, he came up to me—I think we were at the Engine Room in Truro and he came in there and he looked at me, and I played a set or something like that. He was just hanging around and he came over to me and he said—'AJ, you fuckin' cocksucker.' He said—'You finally got it. Now my job is fucked. I'll never get it back again. I'm out of here now. I quit.'"

AJ was right on man and besides, I was so happy when Garry *f*'n said he wasn't ever going to come back again. I mean, that's an awful thing to say about the *f*'n dead, but he had me so *f*'n crazy. Between him and Ricky, I was just a *f*'n basket case.

"But I've got to say about Garry," said AJ. "The first four or five years he was playing around in Halifax or anywhere like that, I'd be there watching him, just to learn. To get it down what Dutchie wanted, because what he played was what Dutchie wanted. He was a good *f*'n drummer. If it wasn't for him, I wouldn't be where I am. Thank God in one way that he *f*'d up, because I got his job.

"What I was learning is that Eastern Canada has their own blues," AJ explained. "What Dutchie does is known as 'the Lunenburg boogie.' There's no other band in Canada, no bands outside of Eastern Canada, that play the style of the blues that we play down here. I don't know how to describe it, really. It's a lot like Chicago blues, but it's got swing. It's got a mixture of everything, of all the different blues because there's no way to describe it, because it's got real nice shuffles to it. The back shuffles. It doesn't have any of that Texas stuff. Nobody here plays that Texas style, but it's got that real swing blues, shuffle, real back beat swing blues and it's just got a real nice, laid-back feel. It's not aggressive, you know. So that's what I was learning and picked up. It's on the beats. The way I describe it is 'on the two and the four.' It's like it's drawn back and it just has that real jazzy-blues swing to it. But don't get me wrong, when the guys want to rock, they can rock too. It's just Dutchie that started it, that's all I can say. Dutchie started his feel of it and his type of blues and you know, he's carried it on and I mean you will hear it in Toronto and you'll hear it out West and a lot of them know if you ask them where they got it, they'll tell you they got it from listening to Dutch Mason. Jeff Healey will tell you that, and all these guys—Kelly James and those guys out in Hamilton— they all do it. When it all comes down to it, they all go back and it really comes back to their main roots. It's all through Dutch Mason."

❊ ❊ ❊ ❊

I see playing with Dutch for the first time as like having your first sexual experience. You don't ever forget it, even though it goes by in a blur. Okay, so there's no applause after sex. But, here I am playing harp in the band of one of the most adored people in Canadian music, loved by blue hairs and people my age and younger. This is the man B. B. King helped nickname "The Prime Minister of the Blues" and I am playing harp in his band. Rick Jeffery told me: "If you've played with Dutchie, it's a sign you've made it." It sure felt like that to me.

❊ ❊ ❊ ❊

We were about halfway from Ottawa to Montreal, the journey to Barrie still lingering in our minds, when Dutch started to nod off.

I'm gonna get some *f*'n sleep.

That's what he said at his acerbic best just before he went to the other side. There was a silence in the car—I was just staring out the window and AJ was concentrating, thankfully, on the road ahead. After about twenty minutes, I decided we'd had enough silence in the El Dorado. I leaned forward from the back seat and undid my belt, talking at a level I was confident wouldn't wake Dutch up.

"Turn the music down a bit, AJ. So tell me, what would you be doing if you weren't playing music?" I couldn't imagine what that might be. He thought for a while, looking in the rear view at me again.

"I used to be a baker," he said, "working for my father-in-law's bakery, but I haven't done much of anything besides playing drums for almost twenty-five years. I started getting into music because my mother played an old pump organ—it's from the 1800s—that dad bought her one time. She played the organ in church in Sydney Mines and she sang in the choir every Sunday, so she was very musical. Mom used to sit there and pump out on that organ. And there was a guy around by the name of Hughie Pickup who was a fantastic piano player. His brother started out with Don Messer and he and his wife were best friends with Don Messer's wife, Naomi, so Messer's drummer, Joe Teonery, and some of the other musicians used to go to their house all the time. Joe taught me how to play with brushes. They'd be over at Hughie's place in Rockingham, outside Sydney, doing like a ceilidh every Sunday night and my mother and father would go over there. I just loved the music and everything, so when I was about twelve years old, I got my father and Hughie to go down to a pawn shop and pick me up a snare drum and I started going over there. This drummer from Don Messer's band, he used to teach me how to use brushes and play all that ceilidh music, Cape Breton music and everything. So I played with them all the time for about a year or two. My father and Hughie would go down, like every Christmas, birthday and that sort of thing and buy me another drum. So by the time I was fourteen, I had a full set, just from picking pieces up at the pawn shop."

"But AJ," I said, "you still take drums back and forth from the pawn shop. They're not the same ones are they?...Sorry man," I said before he could say anything. "I'm just kidding." In the rear view he gave that sheepish smile that he can make when he has done something he shouldn't have and doesn't have any excuse except, "Well, I couldn't help myself, so you have to forgive me." It works every time.

"So then that's when my brother's best friend came up from Windsor one time—John Robie—his family was very musical. He came in and played my mother's organ. He was playing this really nice music. I asked him what it was and he said—'blues'—so that was fine. Then a couple of months later, I was telling him how much I liked it and he came up again to Sydney Mines and brought this album up to me and said— 'Now, this is the music you should be listening to.' The album was James Cotton, his first album. Now this is what I wanted to play. So I listened to that for a while, you know, and finding all these different other albums, but the James Cotton one was my favourite.

"So then John Robie came back up again to hang out with my brother. The second album he brought me was a white band. Then I knew that's the thing I wanted to do. So that went on and on and I kept buying albums like James Cotton, Paul Butterfield and so on. I really liked horn bands, especially after hearing Cotton and Butterfield and all those horns and everything. Then I really liked Blood, Sweat and

Tears and Chicago and whoever else had a blues feel with a rock feel to it—that sort of stuff. I played that stuff in little school bands and everything like that. I did a big drum solo with my high school friends there watching me in the gymnasium. But I stopped playing music when I turned nineteen because I got married and didn't really play. Then I got a divorce and said—'Well, now I can do what I want.' My wife didn't want me playing the whole time I was married. So I'm free, I thought, so I'm going to start playing music."

I wanted to say to AJ that he was free from everything except having to take care of Ellen's cats. I bit my tongue.

✿ ✿ ✿ ✿

We weren't playing the Rainbow Room in the Byward Market until the next night, Tuesday, so we had time to kill.

Carter's van and the El Dorado lost one another somewhere on Bronson Avenue but arrived at the Day's Inn on Rideau, one within a minute of the other, somewhere around four o'clock. The El Dorado caught a few sideways glares as we parked out front of the hotel. I realized that people were staring at us as we got out of the car and walked through the lobby. When I stay in Ottawa on business, no one pays any attention to me. I've got to admit that this feels kind of cool. In comparatively staid Ottawa within two blocks of the Parliament Buildings, the Caddy and the guys in it definitely stood out. After checking in and getting Dutch up to the room where he could have a Marlboro and watch some TV, we took a walk.

Immediately opposite the hotel was a shrine of sorts—Steve's Music. There's one in Toronto and Montreal too, but this was the best of the three I think.

Inside we met Dan Robillard in the guitars section, a late-thirty-ish guy who said he'd been working there for more than a decade and playing guitar in and around Ottawa since he was a kid. He was keen to hear that we played with Dutch, but not mesmerized by the fact. A lot of well-known musicians frequent Steve's. It's one of those places where the staff, a couple of whom still look like throwbacks from the hippie era, make the place what it is. Robillard's hair was cut shorter, but he's part of this feeling too.

"We get everyone in here, from celebrities to moms and pops and the odd aimless wandering psychotic who strolls in from the Market."

He showed Carter and me their selection of Ampegs and a Fender display, gear that's almost exclusively re-issues. We prefer the originals but still, tooling around at Steve's was a treat. And Robillard and his co-workers were characters.

A few minutes later, on Dalhousie Street, my eyes went to an Indian restaurant that wasn't open yet for the day. It was called "The Roses Café Also," which I think is a great name. I was determined to eat there before I left the capital.

In the window of an even more upscale-looking place a block away, there were three or four exotic specials listed on a board, one of which was frog's legs. AJ couldn't resist:

"Hey Dave, what do you think of frogs?"

"What the *f* are you talking about AJ?"

❀ ❀ ❀ ❀

It was just half an hour before the gig and I was nursing a drink at the bar. Carter, Barry and Charlie were tuning up. AJ had gone back to the hotel to get Dutch. The bartender at the Rainbow Room had all kinds of neat stories about the blues musicians he'd met over the years. Dave Wham—I asked him if he knew George Michael, which he didn't find funny—has been working at the Rainbow since the day the doors opened nineteen years ago.

"Next year is our twentieth anniversary," he proclaimed in an astonished way, as if he couldn't believe it himself. But he clearly loves the place. He's poured more than a few martinis, tequila, rum and Jack Daniels, not to mention a whole lot of beer.

The Rainbow Room is on the second floor over top the Rainbow Bistro, on Murray Street on the fringe of the market. The upstairs bar is mostly filled with stand-up bar tables and a five-foot raised stage that was no picnic to tackle with Dutch's wheelchair.

To the left of the stage, there's a huge stone wall that lends something between heritage and grit to the atmosphere. There's also a loft that covers about a third of the main bar floor. In addition to the pictures of many of the musicians who've played there, there are plaques plastered everywhere declaring the Rainbow the Best of Ottawa for entertainment.

Dave Wham introduced me to a silver-haired, mid-fifties guy named Donnie Evans, who was working the door for the night. It was sheer coincidence that he happened to be working the door, because Evans actually played bass with Dutch in Ottawa, and on tours in Ontario and across Western Canada for five or six years, years ago.

"I'll bet Dutch will be happy to see you," I said. There was no doubting Evans was proud of time spent on the road with Dutch. Since people were streaming in, our conversation was cut short as he returned to the cover charge table at the top of the stairs.

"So Dave," I said, "if you've been here since day one you must have been around for most or all of Dutch's gigs."

"I've been here for every gig Dutch has ever played at the Rainbow. He's got his loyal fans here in Ottawa, that's for sure. There are a lot of people in the area from down east. Everyone's always trying to buy him drinks.

"He lights up a room when he walks in. When he comes into the room, it has a different feel. He's a down-to-earth star."

It was fascinating talking to people like Amy Louie and Dave Wham about Dutch. It's one thing to be in the Maritimes and to hear people talk about Dutch. But it's a whole different feeling to be in Toronto and Ottawa talking to people like this about him. I had the strangest urge to document, film or record what they were saying. I felt all the more as if I was in a "Life and Times of Dutch Mason" documentary.

Unfortunately, the bar's main owner, a fellow named Danny Sivyer, was out of town. Dave Wham said Danny was a big Dutch fan too. By the way Dave described him, I got the feeling Dutch and he would feed off each other. Danny apparently does these corny magic tricks, one of which is "the disappearing martini."

"It's a very simple trick, really," says Wham, "but people never get it." I suggested it has to do with simply drinking the martini, but Wham said no. As he laughed about Sivyer's little magic stunts, Wham's admiration for his boss was clear.

In one trick, Sivyer places a cigarette on the top of the bar and rapidly spins his index finger above, the notion being he's creating static electricity and making the cigarette roll away. What people don't watch because they're so fixated on the rotating finger, is the fact that he's gently blowing on the cigarette and making it roll.

The show went well. Ottawa, especially at the Rainbow, is a very knowledgeable city for blues and they know Dutch. One of the biggest blues festivals anywhere in the world takes place in the capital in early

July and Dutch has played there many times. We were fortunate that Tony "D" came down and sat in for a few tunes. Tony is the top dog in Ottawa blues scene, one of the true virtuosos of blues guitar. He has known Dutch and all the guys well for years, having lived for a time in Halifax. His playing is electrifying.

Between sets I was approached by a woman who asked if she could talk to me. She was rather attractive and I was happy to oblige.

"My boyfriend and I play this game. Do you mind if I ask you a few questions?"

"No," I replied. "Ask away."

"We each pick someone out of the crowd and try to guess things about them. Tell me if these things are true. I think you are from the Maritimes."

I interrupted her, saying "Well, I am playing with Dutch, so that's pretty easy to guess."

"I think that you like to sail and that you are a teacher, probably of history."

At that, I was impressed, but I teased her: "Not even close. I teach political science!"

We talked a while longer and after she left, it struck me just how much farther I had to go to be an authentic blues man. She had seen through my "on-the-road" veneer.

❈ ❈ ❈ ❈

As we looped the block after leaving the Days Inn and drove along Dalhousie Street, I realized I never got to "The Roses Café Also" for my Indian food dinner. What we had, of course, was pizza and drinks back in Dutch's room at the Days Inn. The front desk clerk gave us quite an eye when we all straggled in around three-thirty in the morning, along with four or five hangers-on from the gig. They left around six in the morning. Nobody, including Dutch, could remember any of their names.

CHAPTER NINE

Montreal

Tuesday, November 11

All you pretty women, stand in line
I can make love to you baby, in an hour's time
Now ain't that a man
I spell M—A—N
Now ain't that a man.

"I'm A Man," Ellas McDaniel/ Bo Diddley

I wanted to take Dutch to this place in Montreal. "You might have been there before Dutch, but if you haven't I'd like to take you down there. It's on *the Main*, St. Laurent Street."

Oh I *f*'n forgot Dave, you're from here aren't you? But jeez Dave, I've been to St. Laurent, like two hundred *f*'n years ago.

"Yeah, this is where I feel most at home. I figured you've been many times, but I want to take you down to the old part of St. Laurent, below St. Catherine's, to some places I used to hang out."

When I was a kid growing up in Montreal, my mother always told me not to go to *the Main*. "Stay on our side," she would warn me. "Don't go east of Eaton's." If I ever write a book on being English in Quebec in the fifties and sixties, I'm going to call it "East of Eaton's."

I laughed when I told them this, but no one else seemed to get it.

As it turned out, we didn't have time to go down to the Montreal Pool Room. By the time we fought the traffic—and the Quebec construction—and loaded into Café Campus, there was only time to head back to the hotel, get showered, have a drink and make our way up to St. Laurent and Prince Arthur.

Even at nine o'clock the street was buzzing with people, mostly a younger crowd. Café Campus is set off St. Laurent on a pedestrian mall, which adds to the area's festive atmosphere.

Like the Rainbow, Café Campus has an eating area downstairs, and the main bar, which is more of a discothèque, is on the second floor. Above that is a shooter bar. As befitting its name, it always attracts a huge college crowd. They were there for our gig too, but the Dutch alumni skewed the demographic. As in Toronto and Ottawa, there is a Dutch Mason fan club of sorts in Montreal, mostly older fans who have been coming to see him for twenty or thirty years.

The bar was completely black. It was large and cavernous, with thirty-foot-high ceilings, and a fantastic lighting and sound system. The stage was huge compared with most blues stages. There was so much space we didn't know what to do with ourselves. Blues night is traditionally a Wednesday at Café Campus and there's a blues jam that begins every Sunday and goes all afternoon and through the evening.

❖ ❖ ❖ ❖

Even if we didn't get to see parts of St. Laurent, I wished I had had time to visit a personal, favourite place of mine. It's up on Mount Royal, a place where I used to go as a morose teenager to be alone and to think. For anyone who may not know Montreal, on the top of the mountain, facing east and south, is a gigantic cross which is lit up at night. The city always looks small from up there, which makes you feel even more alone.

Although I knew we couldn't get Dutch up there, I told him about it. I had already heard so many of his stories and I was anxious to share some of mine with him. We ended up stumbling across the irony that the same cross was for Dutch, as well, a symbol of personal pain. It was between the second and third sets at Café Campus. We were in a small room with only a couple of chairs, right behind the stage. He was having a smoke and I was sipping a drink that the waitress had brought me. The rest of the guys left to check out the shooter bar on the next level. All I had to do was mention Mount Royal and the illuminated cross.

Let me tell you about me and Montreal. I was loaded all the *f*'n time. Loaded. When I was making that album for London Records. I used to get lobsters from the *f*'n guy, a guy right down outside the hotel here in the city. I was on the fourteenth floor. Outside the hotel right next door was an Italian guy and he used to have live lobsters, there right. So every night I'd phone down when I was making this record. At nighttime, I used to do *f* all, so I'd phone down and say— "Send me five live lobsters." "Yeah, okay Dutch." The guy knew me. Up the *f*'n lobsters would come.

One night I was standing on the balcony out back and I was looking at a *f*'n cross right, and I was thinking to myself, I should *f*'n just jump now, get this *f*'n thing over with, because I'm killing myself. I should just jump and have it over with. I wasn't with Pam or anybody then.

94

I was just alone and that was working on my mind too. I had nobody. Except the guys in the band, who had nobody too, you know what I mean. Anyway, I came back in the living room and I put the lobsters on the *f*'n floor right, and they're crawling all over the floor and I'm patting them and all of a sudden, they got to be my friends. So I phoned Ricky and I said—"Ricky, come up here and get these lobsters, I haven't got the heart to *f*'n boil them up." So he came up and got the lobsters and left. I lost five lobsters thinking they were my friends. So that's how *f*'n crazy I was.

I was at that point where I would have *f*'n hung myself or *f*'n jumped or shot myself or done something because I knew I was heading nowhere. And I was in the middle of making a *f*'n record. For London Records, you know, like The Rolling Stones. I just *f*'d it up, you know, just being me. But anyway, I *f*'n made it through somehow. Like I said the other day. I can't believe I'm still alive. Like I should have been dead twenty-five years ago. I guess when your number is up, your number is *f*'n up, you know.

My mother is ninety—she's in a home, you know—and my father was eighty-six when he died. I guess we've got pretty good genetics, anyway. But I was destroying myself. So when I came home after making that record, I went to my buddy's Kenny Clattenburg's, right, and he picked me up at the airport and he said—"Holy fuck, man." I weighed about 280 pounds and he said—"You look fucking' terrible." I said—"Kenny, I never felt this *f*'n bad in my life." He said—"Well, you'll come home," so he fed *f*'n vitamins to me and the Valium and this and that and I started working out like, see, I had more gout, right, and I started working out and doing this and that and in a month and a half, I was down to 185 and in perfect *f*'n shape. Figure that one out. One month and a half.

"You lost one hundred pounds in a month and a half, Dutch?" I was incredulous. Nobody loses one hundred pounds in a month and a half without dying.

That's right. And here's what I ate. I ate *f*'n tuna and crackers like that and grapefruit juice. That's what I lived off, and tomato soup. That's what I lived off and I worked out every *f*'n day, religiously. And I stopped drinking for a year and a half, just like now. That's when I met Pam, when I wasn't drinking. But I started again and no *f*'n wonder I drove the woman crazy.

❊ ❊ ❊ ❊

It was late as hell when we finished loading out. I talked almost everyone into getting a sausage on a bun from the Slovenian Deli, an old favourite of mine, nearby on St. Laurent. Dutch asked AJ to get him some pizza from a by-the-slice place next door.

I knew St. Laurent was a one-way street, but I wasn't paying attention when AJ pulled out from Prince Arthur heading the wrong way. There was no sign there, plus it was late and there was hardly any traffic—just loads of pedestrians. Carter, Charlie and Barry in the van, immediately behind us, habitually followed the El Dorado onto the street. From out of nowhere, a police cruiser and a van appeared and surrounded us with lights flashing. Four cops milled about the Caddy in two seconds flat. AJ's plea for them to check the out-of-town license plates fell on deaf ears. As did the fact we were with Dutch Mason, which earned only a blank stare. The one officer addressing us was young and cocky, more pre-occupied with seeing if any of us spoke French. He took AJ's and Carter's licenses and the two registrations and disappeared into his cruiser to check us out. The other three cops stood about, trying to decide whether to search us over, especially the van I think. When the cop with the documentation returned, he scanned me and Dutch carefully but waved us on our way—pointing the correct way up St. Laurent. The food was getting cold.

Back at the hotel, Dutch primed himself with another in a seemingly endless string of Marlboros and more stories about Montreal.

Well that was a smooth ƒ'n move AJ, violating the traffic laws of Montreal.

"I should have been watching, Dutch," I said. "I know St. Laurent is one way and I wasn't paying attention. I must be tired."

"Yeah," said AJ. "How the ƒ do I know what's a one-way street in Montreal. It's the most stupid, confusing city I've ever driven in. When we leave tomorrow Dave, you're paying attention."

You know what I ƒ'n think's funny about Montreal now? That it's known for people telling jokes. What's the name of that festival. Not the jazz festival, we played that at the very beginning, I'm ƒ'n talking about the other one.

"Oh the Just For Laughs Festival."

Yeah, that's ƒ'n it. The Montreal Just For Laughs Festival.

"They should hire you for that festival, Dutch. When you tell jokes you sound like Rodney Dangerfield. You even look like him a bit. Tell us a couple."

You mean like, I'll never forget the day I was born, I cried like a baby. Or *f*, did you hear the one about, this guy walked into a *f*'n bar and there was one guy sitting at the bar, right, and there was a girl working behind the *f*'n bar, right, so anyway, the guy walked in and sat down and the other guy sitting at the bar says—"Hey donkey, give me a drink." The girl went and got him a drink and the *f*'n guy says— "What the *f* is this?" So anyway, he did this four or five times—"Hey donkey, get me a drink" So the other guy called her over and he says— "Don't you mind him talking to you like that?" And she says—"No, hee haw always talks to me like that." What a *f*'n stupid joke.

"What about that Charles Manson joke, Dutch?"

Oh yeah, they were interviewing Charles Manson in the cell and they said—"Well, how are you feeling today, Charles?" And he said— "Is it hot in here or am I crazy?"
And what's that other one. Oh yeah, another good *f*'n one was: Is life getting a little dim or am I having another stroke?

"What was it that happened on the subway when you were in Toronto one time?"

Oh yeah. Well, we were on the subway, actually it is a *f*'n joke. We were on the subway and this *f*'n guy had green hair up in the air, and those *f*'n tin things stuck in his ear and face, painted half up and all the ripped-up clothes like something you'd see in *f*'n space, right. I just kind of kept looking at him like that and looking at him and *f*'n guy looked over and he said—"What are you looking at"—or something—

"old man." I said—"It was about twenty years ago, that I ƒ'd a parrot and I was wondering if you were my son."

"The other one is the one you used to say at the end of every show about everywhere you go."

I used to say—"Well, goodnight folks, have a nice night. Remember one thing, wherever you go, that's where you will be and remember one other thing too. You can lead a horse to water but it takes a strong ƒ'n man to drown him." And then—"Drive carefully, because I'm walking." Yeah—"Watch your driving because I'll be walking."

Stupid, ƒ'n foolishness. I used to do Rodney Dangerfield. I used to do Rodney Dangerfield all the time and Ron, Donny's boss, I said "Hey Ron, is that your wife or have you just got a grudge against your cock?"

❊ ❊ ❊ ❊

But speaking of Montreal, Dave, there was one funny thing happened to me here and I was only about eighteen years old. It's a funny ƒ'n story. It was funny to me. I had an old Cadillac and the brakes were going, right, and it was dragging, you know, and the car looked ƒ'n beautiful but the brakes were gone and I said—"Fuck man, we got to stop here somewhere"—so I just happened to stop in front of the Esquire Show Bar and we had not a ƒ'n cent right. So I got out of the car and I'm trying to think—now where are we going to get some ƒ'n money. We got to get some ƒ'n thing. And a voice said—"Dutchie Mason, ain't that a picture." And I looked up and it was a ƒ'n girl, a black girl from Kentville who was a hooker up there and she ƒ'n took us all in the bar and bought us all drinks and loaned us some money and we got a *f*'n place to stay for two or three days and we *f*'d off to Toronto. But wasn't that a fluke. My life is a fluke. Like my life, most of the shit that I've done, I've fluked into it. Now I just got a call or an e-mail a day or two ago from the Montreal Jazz Festival to play up there. I played the first one, like I said. Like I told you, there was just all black guys on the poster and myself. That's just the way it worked out. Big Mama Thornton, John Lee Hooker, B. B. King. That whole bunch I named before.

I remember being here in Montreal once. I was making that *f*'n record, what was it called? "Wish Me Luck." I *f*'n needed luck. "Wish Me Luck" for London Records and when I was making that record, I had a suite at a hotel. That's where they put me up at and I demanded that they had a bar in the studio, so they did. I demanded that. What a *f*'n asshole, you know. So anyway, I had a bedroom, a living room, a kitchen, a bathroom. And in the bedroom, I had a forty-ounce of vodka with a glass and ice. In the living room I had two forties of *f*'n vodka with a glass and ice, and then in the kitchen I had a forty-ounce of vodka with a glass and ice. And I just *f*'n rotated through the suite. But I don't know how much I drank, probably a couple of forties a day. Yeah, I would say in around there being conservative, you know.

It was amazing but it *f*'d me up in so many different ways. It *f*'d me up with my wife. It *f*'d me up with everything. It's just a general *f* up. Booze is the worst. Like it just *f*'d me up, you know what I mean. Now what can you say beyond that.

There was one time we were playing at the Sheraton Hotel in Fort McMurray, Alberta. Prime Time it was called. The first night we were there and the place is sold out and the guy who ran the place—his name was Joe—he brings up a whole tray of B-52's for the band. And

I drank the twenty-four B-52's. Like there's four guys in the band, six each there was supposed to be for the band and I drank the whole twenty-four in the first set. So at the end of the first set, Joe came back and AJ says he told Joe that I wasn't going back out and he asked why. Of course it was because I drank the whole tray and I was loaded. All of a sudden, Joe goes—"Okay, I'll fix this." He walks out to the mike, he says—"Okay people, your money is going to be refunded tonight. Come back tomorrow night, no charge tomorrow night, end of story." We got out of there that night. I couldn't *f*'n believe it.

That was in Alberta and there was a keyboard player there from Fredericton named Stewart MacDougall. We were sitting in this hotel and AJ asked—"Who's that ugly fuckin' guy that Stewart is sitting with? Fuck that guy is ugly," said AJ. So we go—"Stewart, come over." Stewart comes over and we say—"Who the fuck is that ugly guy you're sitting with there?" He goes—"Dutch, that's K. D. Lang. It's a singer, it's a female." Yeah, that was just when K. D. Lang was just starting to make it on Stony Plains Records. Stewart used to be her keyboard player.

CHAPTER TEN

Highway 20, Quebec

Wednesday, November 12

I got 19 kids and they all gotta eat
All 19 I gotta feed
Early this morning I heard a knock on my door
You can't pay the rent, you gotta go.

"Big Boss Man," Al Smith/Luther Dixon

Buzzing along Highway 20 through Quebec, the sign for
Montmagny approached on the right: "Montmagny 47 km." AJ
was adamant we were not staying at the Wigwam Motel or eating at the
Oriental restaurant there, so we kept going toward Rivière-du-Loup.
On the way we passed a couple of speed traps, each with a few cars
pulled over getting tickets.

Getting *f*'n pulled over like that is *f*'n nothing. That was standard
procedure for us whenever Ricky was on the road. He was always
attracting cops, no matter where we went, no matter what time of day.
He had a *f*'n knack for it. That's part of what got to me on the *f*'n road.

Ricky and I both had bad nerves. I was just a *f*'n mess, like, jeez, I thought I was going to *f*'n die, eh. My head was *f*'n all—well I felt *f*'n terrible, just terrible. Nerves are a funny thing, like, you know. But yeah, Ricky had bad nerves too.

"I know he had bad nerves too," I said. "Even recently, I remember a couple of years ago, he said—'Jeez Dave, I don't know if I can talk to you today. I just don't feel like getting out of bed. I just want to pull the covers up over my head and hide.'"

And *f*'n die, yeah. I know how he felt. Yeah, I know how he *f*'n— well, him and I were best of *f*'n buddies, eh, you know. He was with the heroin and me with the *f*'n Valium and the booze and that, you know.

I mean, I started out, I drank a lot—a lot—and just, fuck, I don't know, just progressed on to drinking and taking *f*'n pills and trying to *f*'n carry on through *f*'n life, you know. But my morning *f*'n thing would be I'd take about four Valium and two big drinks and then I'd start my *f*'n day, you know. That's how I was in the end, you know. But if I didn't have *f*'n Valium, I'd be *f*'d. I'd be screwed. Now it's not Valium, it's Xanax. But my nerves were so *f*'n bad, and if you've ever had those *f*'n panic attacks like that, like you feel like you're going to die. I mean you just *f*'n feel like you're going to die, you know.

Some of it could have been from the pressure of being the band leader. I don't know. I never really bothered to try and figure it out, like, why my nerves were so bad. They were just *f*'n bad, you know.

And Jesus Christ, the panic attacks are just the *f*'n worst. Like your heart seems to stop. You can't focus on anything like that and oh, my, fuck. It's just the worst, the *f*'n worst.

"I've often wondered how you do it Dutch. I remember one time you were playing at the Rebecca Cohn Theatre, with the symphony orchestra and Theresa and Matt Minglewood were playing as well. You were the headliner and I ran into you at Your Father's Moustache at two o'clock in the afternoon. I was there for Joe Murphy's Saturday Jam. You kept taking twenties out and saying to the bartender—'Just pour the vodka into the glass until the twenty is used up'—and then another twenty would come out. I sat with you for about an hour at the bar and you went through about sixty bucks' worth of vodka. And you had been drinking before I got there and then I left and you were still sitting at the bar.

"But now you hardly drink at all, if ever, even though your fans are always trying to buy you drinks. They seem to like it when you get drunk and do crazy things. I guess it reminds them of the old days when they would come and see you play. They don't want to get older and they don't want you to grow up either."

That's right.

CHAPTER ELEVEN

Edmundston

Thursday, November 13

I'm gonna move up to the country, I'm gonna paint my mailbox blue
I'm gonna sit on my front yard, woman, I'm gonna wait for a letter from you
I'm gonna move down to Florida, where the sun shines every day
I'm gonna find me a little girl and lay down in the sand and play

"Gonna Move Up To The Country," Taj Mahal

The Madawaska francophones, the Brayonne as they're called, are neither purely Acadian nor purely Quebecois. Life has always been hard in The Republic of Madawaska. The forest industry is the main source of employment and, like people everywhere who work long hours, they love to party. Their June Foire Brayonne is a festival of such growing popularity that bands are clamoring for a chance to play. I was there once with Theresa. We were treated like royalty by the local organizers, and the fans just go nuts over the music. Although this is November and not the Foire Brayonne, we knew we would have a great crowd.

O'Costigan's is a new place, decorated completely in black, like Café Campus, with a less elaborate but still decent light and sound system. It's also smaller than the Montreal bar. With Dutch in town, again the demographic shifted radically. The crowd gets a lot older, but it's still a party for everybody. It is the only place I've ever seen or heard of where the stage is actually propped above one of the bars. It looked as though vertigo could be a problem for Dutch and for me too, as neither of us like heights. We wondered how we were ever going to get Dutch up there, but after some maneuvering, it worked out. I couldn't help worrying about what we'd do if there was ever a fire.

Back at the Howard Johnson's, just two blocks away, we grabbed a drink before the gig. The guys were either watching TV or showering, or like AJ, finishing their hair. I didn't want to stay in my room—I roomed with Carter for the whole trip—because he was watching TV with the radio on again. The routine on the road is always the same. We check into the hotel, go to our room, pour a drink and watch TV sitting up in bed. The Simpsons is always the first choice, or a re-run of an old comedy show. After that, it's anything but the news. I have tried to watch TV and listen to country music at the same time but after a while I just can't stand it any more. It's like two voices telling you something different in each ear—Homer Simpson eating donuts in one and Waylon Jennings singing in the other.

When you are on the road with Dutch, you can always go to his room. He hardly sleeps—it cuts down on his smoking time—and he is always up for a chat.

It was just the two of us now, so I asked Dutch about more things, like when he got started and about getting married. It doesn't really matter what you ask him, he just loves to talk about the way things were. When Dutch tells his stories, it's as if he were holding court. He lies back in bed with one arm crooked behind his head and off he goes. His audience is really just that, an audience. I think this way of speaking must develop with being famous. Everyone always wants to hear him tell of his wild days on the road—I certainly can't resist—and Dutch obliges. The conversation, though, is always one-sided. The stories, I think, are also masks. Dutch will tell anyone about what he's done; even crazy and embarrassing events are recounted without a hint of self-consciousness. But the real soul of the man is kept much more carefully concealed.

Sometimes the stories jumble in and out and weave over one another. But even when they're a bit hard to follow because of names you may not know or the chronology seeming out of context, they are always crazily spell-binding.

❋ ❋ ❋ ❋

This is how *f*'n stupid I am. I was in Moncton one time and I went in the bank, the Bank of Commerce. I went into the Bank of Commerce because the guy that we were playing for paid us in a cheque. I went into the bank, put the cheque down and signed it and everything *f*'n like that and the money started coming across the thing. I said— "Don't you want to see any ID?" She says—"Don't you remember me at all?" It was my ex-wife, Ginny. My first *f*'n wife and I didn't remember her. That's how *f*'n stupid I was, you know. Not paying attention, you know.

"Didn't you have more than one wife who worked at a bank, Dutch?" I'd heard pieces of this before, chunks of his marital history described at two, three or four o'clock in the morning, after gigs, but never all in one sitting, threaded together into a single yarn.

Yeah, there was my second wife, Frances. When I was with Frances, that was a constant *f*'n fight because she was really, really pretty, eh, and all the guys would be *f*'n around with her and I would be fighting with this and that guy, it was stupid *f*'n kid stuff, you know. I never should have done it [the fighting], you know. When did I marry her, *f*, I don't know, well, it was 1964 or 1962, in around there. I married her in Toronto, right at Bathurst Street. She was working in the bank up in Toronto and yeah, I married her in Toronto. I don't even know how *f*'n long we were married. I can't remember because we'd be together, apart, together, apart, together, apart like that, I don't even know. She died too, eh. Fuckin' sin you know. She was a nice woman.

We were never together that *f*'n long enough to even call it a marriage, you know. We'd be together, then we'd be apart, oh my fuck. It's just hard on the *f*'n nerves, eh. I started taking Valium when I was twenty-one and that didn't even *f*'n work that good, so one of my buddies next door to me when I was living in Aldershot, just outside of Kentville, said here have a drink for *f*'s sake. Anyway, I took a couple of these Valium and had a drink and *f* I felt great. And that's what started me *f*'n drinking. Never drank before that. I hated drinking and I started drinking then and I never *f*'n stopped until, well I'm almost stopped now. But I *f*'n felt great. So that's how I started drinking, my nerves were so *f*'n bad, really, really *f*'n bad.

I don't know why they were so bad. I really don't *f*'n know. Probably from everything. Not having any money, being *f*'n married, not wanting to *f*'n be married, not working enough, you know, every *f*'n thing in general like, you know. Just life in general, you know.

"So, did you ever feel like you wanted a home, Dutch?"

Fuck Dave, didn't make a *f*'n bit of difference to *f*'n me. I could live anywhere. Yeah, I could live—well, look where I'm living now. I could live any *f*'n where now, didn't make any difference.

I did for a while after I met Pam. I came back after making the album for London Records and played here and there, went out on the road again and I met Pam out west—I met her in Vancouver— and then when I came back, I said I should *f*'n settle down a little bit here, like you know, try to get things straight, but I *f*'d all that up too through drinking.

"When did you marry Pam, Dutch? She's a very lovely person."

Oh *f*, I don't know. Don't ask me, I don't know. I can't remember when it was. She'd remember. I was forty-three, so figure it out. And then Garrett was born a year later because she—I'll tell you how that worked. She didn't even know it and neither did I, but she was pregnant when we got married, but we didn't know that. She said, "Jeez, I've been sick every morning." I said you better go to the doctor and find out what the *f* is wrong with you, like go. So she went and she said "Jeez, I'm pregnant." I went, we just got married in time. Yeah, that's what *f*'n happened. We didn't know.

And all three women worked in the same bank. They all worked in the same bank, Bank of Commerce. I met Pam in a bank. So anyway, that was that and then she came back to Nova Scotia and we got married. Then I had a home and all that stuff. Went through all the *f*'n bullshit and I made a whole load of *f*'n money and blew it all like I do every *f*'n thing in my life and I mean it'll just go on and on forever until I *f*'n die and that'll be the end of it, you know. That's just the way things go.

It made me think that there is a whole other side to Dutch. We only ever see the performer and the man who could out-drink the devil himself. We don't really ever get to see the husband puttering around the house or the father playing ball or going to a parent-teacher meeting.

Dutch told me once about going to see Garrett's teachers. I forget the details but I could never lose the image of Dutch talking to a teacher about punctuality or sitting up straight in class. Pam told me that Dutch was a good father. Although being on the road meant being away from home for considerable stretches of time, he was also, most of the time, a full-time dad, something not all children get to experience. Still, the image of Dutch sitting in one of those half-sized grade school desks talking to "Miss Honey" about his son's homework is a funny one.

CHAPTER TWELVE

Fredericton

Friday, November 14

Every day, baby
When the sun goes down
I get with my friends
And I begin to drown
I don't care
What the people are thinkin'
I ain't drunk
I'm just drinkin'

"I Ain't Drunk," Jimmy Liggins

It was weird coming off the road and being back in Fredericton to play at Bugaboo Creek. I've played a lot here with Theresa and Dutch, usually with AJ arriving at the very last second from Halifax, and with Carter who has to drive him, wait for him, pick up his drums, help him find Ellen's cats, all the while gritting his teeth in frustration.

Sue decided she wanted to cook a meal for the band and so when we got into Fredericton, the boys checked into the Lord Beaverbrook Hotel and I hopped into a taxi to see Sue and especially Riiko. As much as you might miss your spouse, there is no pain like that of being separated from your child.

I could also hardly wait to get home with all the stories I had to tell. Sue had been cooking half the day and the familiar smells evoked a thousand happy memories. I told the guys to get to my place by five-thirty to give us time to visit before we ate and to digest before we played.

Dinner at our place has become a tradition for AJ, Carter, Charlie and Barry, although this was the first time Dutch came over. The Caddy drew a few stares from my neighbors as the guys pulled up in my driveway, which Dutch noticed and laughed about.

You've got some spies in your neighbourhood, Dave.

Sue likes to prepare a meal for the band in part because she enjoys the company—"What a strange *f*'n woman she is" Dutch would say—and in part because having a brother who was a musician, she knows what a home-cooked meal and a few hours away from the hotel room can mean. I know that the band always looks forward to the hospitality.

The guys have been coming over often enough that they have their own routines. Barry sits at the breakfast counter in the kitchen. Carter sits on the sofa and plays with our Golden Retriever. Charlie gets a beer, sits off to the side and works on a crossword puzzle, making him the only one on the road who regularly buys the newspaper. AJ loves to cook, so he pours himself a rum and coke and hovers around Sue and the stove.

As always, dinner was an event. We had vegetarian lasagna with oven roasted vegetables—but no mushrooms. Sue told Carter she'd made stuffed mushrooms especially for him. Of course, everyone knows he's allergic to them. For the guys, it was "a night in Provence" you might say. We had sausages, Caesar salad and lots of French bread for Barry. As happens when people are seriously engaged in eating, there were periods of silence as the food was wolfed down, interrupted by intermittent bursts of thanks and congratulations to Sue for the great food.

Musicians on the road have their special eating patterns. Like bears, they can go for long periods without eating and follow this with huge intakes of food. Dutch doesn't eat all that much, but little Barry can really pack it in, especially the dessert, which, following tradition, is chocolate chip cookies. He wrapped a few up in a napkin for after the gig.

As is typical of the Japanese, the meal must not only be a delight to the taste but to the eyes as well. Everything was very carefully laid out—a far cry from a pizza box resting on the TV and the band all sitting around Dutch's bed eating with our fingers and washing it down with beer. At the house, of course, we have wine glasses and side plates and salad bowls and cups with saucers for our coffee. The deliberateness and propriety with which the dinner was presented brought out the best manners in everyone, as does Sue's hosting. We all felt a bit like Tom Sawyer, scrubbed and proper for Sunday school.

The conversation was, as usual, patterned and repetitious. The same jokes and stories came out—they never fail to make us laugh. Yet there is always something new to add to our repertoire of stories. AJ came upstairs just before we ate—as was customary he brought his laundry over—and was rubbing his ear. He continued doing this during the meal.

"What's wrong," I asked. "Is the stuffing in your head starting to come out?"

"Well, the thing is, I was using a Q-Tip this morning and I think the end might have come off in my ear."

"Might have? How can you not know?"

"Sue," said AJ, "could you take a look in my ear?"

Sure enough, after some examining, Sue declared that indeed he had a Q-Tip in his ear. She gave him some pointers on how to get it out. Dutch was laughing.

Just like a ƒ'n Seinfeld episode! Like a ƒ'n TV show. Just a lot of ƒ'n foolishness about nothing. A ƒ'n Q-Tip in his ear!

The medical treatment AJ got from Sue seemed to give Dutch an idea. His arthritis has damaged his fingernails and he wanted to know if there was anything that could be done about it. Dutch absolutely hates going to the doctor, but having Sue right there gave him the chance to get medical advice without the anxiety of a trip to the office. After Sue told him what might work, he looked at her and then pointed at me.

Why the ƒ are you with that ƒ'n guy? What about me? Ain't I some kind of a ƒ'n good catch?

That became the running gag for the night at Bugaboo Creek. After every second or third song, Dutch would look at Sue and give her a smile that said—*Why not me?* And then he would ask her over the mic if she wanted to drop me and go with him.

Bugaboo Creek was like a second home to me I've played there so often in the past eight years. Setting up is routine. No need to try to figure out how much space each of us has or where the electric outlets are, or how the PA works. For musicians, the stage is their workplace and its intricacies and quirks become second nature. Bugaboo has a railing on each side of the bar, just the perfect place to put my rum and coke. Most of the time you have to put your drink on your amp, which is convenient enough, but everybody knows someone who has accidentally dumped their beer down the back of their amp and either ruined it or given themselves a real jolt.

Dutch on stage these days is not like the past. In his heyday, he was a robust figure at the mic, one of Canada's greatest blues guitar players. Now that he has to perform in a wheelchair, everything has changed. The mic stand is brought down to a comfortable level and AJ adjusts the monitors because Dutch is quite particular about them. He wants to hear himself well. At Bugaboo, I got him a stool so that his cigarettes and ashtray were close by. Another stool was set for his beverage—vodka when he was drinking, now replaced with water or coffee—and his Kleenex, which he arranged so that they were within reach.

Dutch's peculiar style is to play very long songs. The other band I play with is Fredericton's George Street Blues Project. We play twelve to fourteen songs per hour set. Dutch might play five or six. This is because he likes to give everyone a chance to solo. He is in no hurry to bring the song to an end. I've been told that in the old days, "Who Do You Love" or "Bo Diddley" could go on for twenty or thirty minutes. He makes room for long solos, which give him a chance to light a new cigarette, to chat with someone in the audience and to enjoy the band as they play.

Between sets he mingles with the audience, making sure that everyone who wants to say hi gets his undivided attention at least for a few moments. Dutch is also careful to make sure that any players he recognizes in the audience get an invitation to sit in with the band. Huey York would always get up with us and sing a few country tunes or an Elvis number. Huey passed away last year and we all miss him, especially Dutch. In Fredericton, Dave Smith, an old friend of Dutch's and a brilliant blues and jazz guitarist, was down for the show. He got up, which was a treat, but a difficult challenge because, like all jazz players, he knows so many damn chords. Dan Robichaud also got up and played some tunes on the harp. I know how much he admires Dutch and sitting in Rick's spot was a thrill for him.

Tearing down the gear was a little more exhilarating than the same old routine of packing things in and heading to a hotel. It was knowing that I'd be with my family. And there was the usual chatting with the hangers-on, most of whom are friends of mine. Like Ricky and AJ, I had that extra strut in my stride that comes from being associated with the Prime Minister of the Blues. It was a chance to really feel cool on my home turf.

CHAPTER THIRTEEN

Saint John

Saturday, November 15

Sloooooo Fried Baloney, I've gotta have some
Sloooooo Fried Baloney, yes it tastes good
Sloooooo Fried Baloney, give it to me,
Let me tell you about Slo Fried Baloney
We eats it on the road, we eats it at home
We eats it all the time because I love Slo Fried Baloney

"Slo Fried Baloney," Barry "Scrapper" Stevenson

I was grateful for the day at home. I had kept up as best I could on the road, but it just wasn't the same as being home. I'd missed hearing about Riiko's science homework, how her last swim practice went and about how things were at work for Sue.

❖ ❖ ❖ ❖

Saint John is only an hour's drive from Fredericton, so everyone slept in and relaxed at the hotel. When I rejoined them with a tray of Tim Hortons coffee in hand, Charlie was busy doing his crossword puzzle, Carter was watching TV and listening to music on the radio with Barry.

AJ and Dutch, who was propped up in bed, were reliving more of the old days. AJ flitted around him like a mother hen. They were a pair of old friends who knew each other's thoughts and moods with an uncanny anticipation.

By the time we got to Saint John, it was late afternoon and the sun was just starting to go down. We would have plenty of time to get to the bar and drop off our gear before checking into the hotel. I still liked to get there early, just to be sure, but Dutch said to me, as he had before:

Fuckin' relax Dave, we'll get there alright.

And sure enough, of course, we always did.

Saint John is a good blues town. You cannot always count on a big crowd, but those who come out are enthusiastic. Melvin's, where we were playing, has its regular customers who know both the blues and the members of the band. It was nice to see familiar faces. We also hoped to run into the guys from the Hill Brothers Band, a fixture in Saint John and among the best players anywhere in Canada. Dutch looked forward in particular to seeing Steve Hill, the band's singer, who has inherited Ricky's mantle as the best harp player in these parts. Dutch wanted Steve to sit in for a while.

There is a culturally determined etiquette in the blues world about sitting in, almost like a mating dance, that completely envelops all the participants. Here are the rules. First of all, it's rude to ask if you can get up and sit in for a few tunes, unless you are very good friends. In fact, being able to ask to sit in without violating the norms is a sign of close friendship and, much like a promise ring, cements a relationship. This rule holds true regardless of the different status the players have within the blues world. It would be as rude for me to ask to sit in with a novice band as it would be with a top touring act if I did not know them well. Secondly, and this is the flip side, the performing musician is obligated to invite his or her peer to play a few tunes. It is rude not to offer. You always extend the invitation. The harmonica player in the band is expected to ask the harmonica player in the audience, the drummer their fellow drummers, and so on. However, it is important that the invited musicians never over-stay their welcome. The code is clear. The band member usually has the say over who can sit in, during what song and for how long, unless they are themselves not a permanent part of the band. So when I play with Theresa Malenfant, I can decide if someone is going to sit in. With Dutch, though, I am a fill-in for Ricky, so it's proper for me to ask Dutch first if someone can get up. How many songs the person gets to play depends on their status. If they are a relative newcomer, they will get up for one song, two at most. Steve Hill is the top harmonica player in the Maritimes—along with Joe Murphy— so I am expected to let him play as long as he wants.

Friends often ask me how blues players can get up and join in another band without knowing or rehearsing the material. The answer has partly to do with the nature of blues music and partly the economics of the blues scene. Blues has a standard repertoire that most experienced players know. As well, the common chord structures, such as eight- or twelve-bar songs, make it easy to pick up the movement of the song. A small cue might be given, such as AJ telling Steve that the next song is a swing shuffle in C. Often the drummer or bass player will help the player if there are stops or unexpected changes. Mostly though, you have to play with your eyes and ears wide open and hope for the best.

All blues players can get up and jam like this because blues is by economic necessity an improvised musical form. Being in a band consumes a lot of time. Most shows last from ten o'clock until two o'clock in the morning. Setting up takes an hour as does tearing down. Driving to the gig also takes time. For this, for all the years of practice, for the broken strings that need replacing, and amp repairs and expensive vintage guitars, you might earn $125 each per night. It's hard to justify endless days of practice on top of this, especially when there is rent to pay and kids to feed. So if you want to make it in blues, you have to be able to jump in and play with a minimum of rehearsal.

The show at Melvin's started as all the previous gigs had. We began with an instrumental that Carter had written, one that he recorded on the CD we had done together. Then Charlie Phillips sang a tune, one of my favourites, "Goin' Up The Country," by Canned Heat. Then Charlie introduced Dutch as he always does—"Let's hear it folks for Dutch Mason!" as the band began the opening riff of "Walkin' Blues." "Let's hear it for the Prime Minister of the Blues, Mr. Dutch Mason!" There was always someone to help Dutch wheel through the crowd and onto the stage. The band stayed on the one riff until Dutch gave us the signal to start cycling through the chord changes so he could begin. The crowd at Melvin's cheered, as they do everywhere, when Dutch started to sing.

So went every set on the trip. Now that he can only sing, Dutch calls out the songs, choosing them as he goes. In the old days, when he still played guitar, he would finish each song with a guitar flourish and as he was doing it, imperceptibly slide to a new key, starting the riff of the next song without a breath. Knowing the order of the songs and how Dutch started each one, the band would simply join in. This seamlessness was one of the trademarks of Dutch's bands.

At Melvin's, Steve got up and played most of the second set, much to the delight of the audience. His playing is much more energetic and exciting than mine. I've been a sideman my whole career, always just filling in and accenting the singer and the guitar player. Steve, though, leads his own group and so has to provide the energy and drive for the whole band, using the harmonica as his fuel. As it was with Ricky, it is always inspiring, always a learning experience, to be around and to watch and listen to performers like Steve Hill.

The night ended with Steve and I chatting about technique and about gear, with the buzz of tearing down going on around us. When we play with Dutch we always try to hurry because these days he is often in pain at the end of three sets, and he is anxious to get back to the hotel, where he can get comfortable in bed and relax from the stress of performing and meeting people.

Back at the hotel following the gig, what I think used to be a Keddy's and is now a Coastal Inn up by Fort Howe, Dutch was naked as usual on his bed. I was getting used to seeing Dutch's balls; one can get used to anything I suppose.

There was a time we were out west when it wasn't me who was running around half naked. You tell about it AJ. I wasn't even *f*'n there. I was waiting with Al, our manager, three hours up the highway, thinking—"Oh, what the *f*, they're going to be late. We're not going to make Calgary on *f*'n time."

"Okay," said AJ. "I'll never forget this. So what happened, it was hot, it was the first week of August in 1983—this was my second month with Dutchie, when we were first going on the road and we were going across the prairies, from Winnipeg to Calgary and we were outside of Regina, and there was Dale White and I and Rick and Terry Edmonds and we had this Aries station wagon and we had the back seat down and there was Terry and Ricky in the back seat, just in their underwear, laid out on blankets in the back and everything, in the back with the seat down and there was Dale and I in the front. Dale had his New York City police cop hat on, in his underwear; the blue underwear with the white stripes on them.

"I just had my underwear on too and it was so hot. We had all the windows open, no sun roof, no air conditioning. We had the back windows down and we were sweating and to top it off, I was speeding because we were thinking—'twenty-four hours, holy shit man, we got to get out to Calgary.' So outside of Regina, all of a sudden, I was going about 120-130 anyway and red lights come up behind the car and the cops pull us over and I go—'oh no, here we go.' We got no seat belts on, no shoes on, I'm driving in my underwear and we got the RCMP pulling us up.

"The guy comes up to the door and he said—'holy shit, what are you guys doing?' We said—'well, it's hot.' He said—'I know, but what are you guys doing?' At first he sees four guys just with no shirts on. He thought we were a bunch of nudists coming from a nudist camp. He said—'well, you know why I stopped you,' and I said—'why?' I guess probably I hoped it was for speeding and he said—'well, yes, but you know you're not supposed to be driving with no shoes on. You don't have any shoes on, you guys in the back laying down, you're supposed to be in the back seat with seat belts on. You're laying in the back seat.' He said—'why are you in such a hurry?' And I said—'well, we're going to a gig; we're in a band,' and he said—'what's the name of the band?'— and I said—'The Dutch Mason Blues Band.' He said—'Oh, yeah.' I said—'we got to be in Calgary and everybody told us it's going to be twenty-four hours, we got to be in Calgary by tomorrow night and we just left Winnipeg.' He said—'well, just a minute.' He said—'I got to go back and call into the office.'

"So we're sitting there, oh my god, and you know this is wasting time.

Al's waiting, Al and Dutchie are waiting for us about three hours up the road. He gives us money for four hours worth of gas, he gives us just enough money for gas to get us four hours because they want to make sure they don't lose us. Dutchie and him are in a big one-ton truck, Dutchie and Al, the road manager.

"And we're in the station wagon, so we're going—'okay, now this is taking us a half hour. Al is going to think we skipped off on him or we went ahead of them. Now they're going to be pissed off.' So anyway, this takes fifteen to twenty minutes. The cop comes over to the car and we're thinking—'okay, now what's he going to do?'

"He says—'okay, I was just talking to my dispatcher, the sergeant there or the corporal or whatever he is, the head fellow at the Regina office. First I was going to give you a speeding ticket, but I'll tell you this. This is what my boss told me to do. He said to tell you guys to slow down. He said it's only sixteen hours to Calgary, so he said to take your time, and he wants to know if Dutchie still does "Slo Fried Baloney" and when is he going to come and play Regina again.' And we just said—'what?' And he said—'my dispatcher is from Windsor, Nova Scotia. He grew up with Dutchie and he wants to know if he's still playing "Slo Fried Baloney," and when is he coming to town?' And I said—'oh my god.' As a matter of fact, he scratched out the ticket and he just put down a warning and that was it. That's what we done."

❖ ❖ ❖ ❖

AJ loves to tell this story because it shows how important you are when you play in the Dutch Mason Blues Band. It was the first time he real-ized what a big deal it was. Twenty years later, he hasn't lost the elation and self-worth that comes from being Dutch's drummer. That *is* who he is. It will be his epitaph—"HERE LIES AJ: DUTCH'S DRUMMER."

The first time I heard "Slo Fried Baloney," I thought it was "Oh, What A Feeling" or some other familiar tune. It's a hard-driving number with lots of horns and with Dutch at his grittiest, James Brown yelps and all. Dutch not only sings the regular lyrics but all sorts of improvisational lines. When he's done, you come away believing that Dutch really does love baloney. I mean, really, really loves it.

After AJ's story, I insisted we play the tune from Dutch's *Special Brew* album. After the main segment of the song, Dutch breaks into a rambling chatter:

Oooo, you know I'm gonna tell you the story, about baloney.
Yes! Huh! You know, we eats it on the road and we eats it at home.
As a matter of fact, we eats it all the time, because I loooove baloney. Yeah!
I love it, I love it, I love it, I love it! Oooo!
I likes baloney. I've got to have some.
I get lonely without baloney. Humph! Huh!
Sloooooo fried baloney. Ow! Gonna take some baloney.
Slooooooo fried baloney, it tastes good!
Sloooooo fried baloney, give me some. I'm gonna take it.
You know what I'm gonna do? I'm gonna put some in a fryin' pan and I'm
gonna cook it up. I'm gonna throw it in the pot, I'm gonna boil it up.
I'm gonna take some of that, gonna throw it on the floor
and I'm gonna pick it up
and I'm gonna eat it, because it tastes good and I love baloney, son.
I love it, I love it, I love it, I love it, I love it. I got to have it, I got to have it.
I'm going to shove some down my throat, drop it on my shoes, stick it on my
face, rub it down the side of my pants. I love it!
I got to have it—give it to me!

When I hear this song I'm reminded of the scene in the deli from *When Harry Met Sally* where Sally is showing Harry, very graphically, what a fake orgasm sounds like. The elderly woman in the next booth turns to the waiter after Sally has climaxed and says: "I'll have whatever she had." I kinda feel the same way about baloney—or is it bologna—after hearing what it does to Dutch.

❊ ❊ ❊ ❊

I said to Dutch, "I don't understand about being naked all the time. I'm Catholic and when I was a kid we all believed that the nuns took showers with their habits on. I close the door to the bathroom even when I'm home alone."

I just don't like wearing clothes and when I decide to take all my *f*'n clothes off, that would be it. If anybody *f*'n came, that would be up to them.

"Like that time where you were exposed playing at the supper club. Wasn't that at the Royal York, in the Imperial Room or something?"

No, it was a place called Lucifers, in Calgary. It was a big *f*'n sit down. It was a night club but it was a *f*'n supper club too and I fell off the *f*'n stage backwards and *f*'n hit the wires and the PA all *f*'n fell down and everything. I never even wore any undershorts, eh. I was walking backwards, looking at *f*'n Fish and I just walked off the stage and I was drunk too, eh, so I got back up on the stage and jeez, my pants were ripped and my nuts were hanging down and I'm trying to push them back up and put my legs together and every *f*'n thing.

It was quite a sight. And a girl came up on stage and grabbed my nuts and pushed them up inside my pants and said just keep your legs together. I said—"Thanks."

"You said—'thanks'—as though someone was handing you the butter across the table?" I was laughing of course. "I've heard that that wasn't the only time you were ever exposed on stage."

Oh yeah, we were playing the day that Elvis Presley *f*'n died. We were playing at the Grand Hotel in Bridgeport, Ontario, right in Bridgeport. Anyway, these two big *f*'n truckers said—"Play something by Elvis." I said—"Leave the man alone. I'm not playing anything by him."

So I took my clothes off for no *f*'n reason, right. No reason, I just took my clothes off, so then everybody in the band took their clothes off, right. So we played the whole first *f*'n set with no clothes on, then we put our clothes back on and finished the set.

The audience cheered, some of them went—"Oooooo," like the girls and then they kept looking again and they didn't say anything after that and then these two big *f*'n truckers wanted to *f*'n beat me up and I said—"Hey pal, you can beat me up, do whatever, but why don't you get up and sing an Elvis song and I'll play the *f*'er." The next *f*'n night, you couldn't get in the *f*'n bar, it was so packed.

We played there one week a month at this bar. People would be like—"Take your clothes off, take your clothes off!"—you know, we incited them into that, like you know. But my God it was *f*'n funny the first time we did it.

We used to play there all the time and Stan, the guy that owned the *f*'n place, here's what he would do. I would knock on the door upstairs, his office like, at three in the morning, right and I'd go—"Stan," and he'd go—"Dutch," and I'd go—"Yeah." "Click" the door would open about that far and a hand would come out with a forty-ounce of dark rum on the end of it. I'd just take the bottle and say—"Good night, Stan." He'd say—"Good night, Dutch." That's the way it *f*'n went, eh.

Then one night we were at the Wyse Owl in Dartmouth, I just dropped my *f*'n pants and played a half a set with no *f*'n pants on and stuff like that, just foolish stuff, you know. Who the *f* would do that now? Give me a break.

CHAPTER FOURTEEN

Moncton

Sunday, November 16

Ain't got time to buy flowers
Yeah, ain't got time to make a date
Yeah, I can't sit down to have breakfast
Because you know I stay up too late
Well I ain't got time for romancin'
I gotta get it and I gotta get it quick
So I guess you're gonna see
That's the way it's gonna be
Wham, bam, thank you Ma'am

"Wham, Bam, Thank You Ma'am," Rick Jeffery

The Salisbury Irving Big Stop was pretty familiar-looking turf, almost a sign of reassurance that all was well with the world. Everyone had a hot turkey sandwich in the restaurant there except Dutch, who ordered another plate of scallops as he had on the first day of the tour. It was the middle of the afternoon, but at the Big Stop, it doesn't matter. It's as busy at three in the afternoon as it is at six or ten o'clock.

We attracted quite a bit of attention when we went in, a couple of truckers recognizing Dutch and coming over to say hello. One got him to autograph an Irving napkin, which he carried away proudly.

Carter told AJ and I what he wanted off the menu and he went out to the CD rack in the Mainway store, to check out the country music selection. Blues players almost always love country music too. I could barely hear Dutch over the din of the restaurant clamor.

We had a guy, Al "Silk" Barrett; he was the road manager.

"This is the same guy you were with on the road out west when you were waiting for AJ and Ricky and the guys?" I asked. "The day they got stopped by the cops with only their underwear on?"

Yeah, that's the guy, Al. He made all the arrangements for the hotels and stuff like that and I did half the booking and then the booking agency did the other half of the bookings like that. Al was the only *f*'n guy that I know who would be our *f*'n roadie. He set up the PA, set up the lights, fixed everything, *f*'n did everything. Kept care of the *f*'n money, did everything.

I'd just go down to Al at the end of the week and say—"Got a couple of grand?"—and he'd go—"Yeah, here, I'll write it down in the book." That's the way it was done. I never asked Al once in my life how much money he made.

"Dutch, are you saying you had a road manager who you were paying and you didn't know how much money he made?"

Not a *f*'n clue, never asked him. I just said—"Go ahead, you handle it, there you go." He would just hand me money if I needed money for something, for this or that. He would hand me the *f*'n money and away I would go. I never asked him.

When it started we were sometimes making like two hundred dollars apiece a week, then it was three hundred and then it was a thousand a week apiece and then when we started making money, we were making like ten, twelve, fifteen grand a week. Then all the band was on salary so I was making all the *f*'n money. They'd be making maybe five hundred a week per guy, but we also included their guitar strings, sticks, drum heads, everything included.

I remember Ricky had a garbage bag, a green garbage bag full of *f*'n harps, just full of harps. I said—"What's that Ricky"—and he said—"They're harps, but they're no good right" and I said—"Well they better start getting good because we're losing *f*'n jobs and I can't pay as much." All of a sudden he got the bag out with the harps all over the floor fixing them. So that's the way if *f*'n went.

But you know, I spent money on everything. On anything I could spend it on. I bought a van for the band, a street van loaded, like it had air, tilt, cruise, *f*'n everything. I bought that for the band and I bought a car for the band too. Both two brand new cars. I bought a *f*'n brand new Imperial and a four-wheel drive, two more brand new cars, so I had four cars on the go and then they complained about the van—"There's not enough foot room in here"—so I went—"I can't *f*'n win." One time, Al said to buy one of them *f*'n electric light *f*'n trucks that you see with a steel floor in it. He said—"Just put them in that because that's what the van is going to look like in two *f*'n months anyway." And of course it did.

And see, that's from being friends, you know, like you're real good *f*'n friends. Like I said once to Blair—"You're fired." He said—"You can't fire me." I said—"What? You're fired." He said—"You can't fire me. I'm not leaving." I just turned around and walked out of the room. What the ƒ do you say to that. I just went—"Okay." So that was that.

But eventually, here's how the band broke up.

"Was this back around 1980 when you were supposed to have retired?"

Dave, here's how I had to break the band up, so we'd still be friends. I said—"Boys"—we were in Campbellton and they'd just smashed up a hotel room and wrote off a car while they were there. They were smashing up bottles and breaking out windows and tearing the toilets apart, just kids ƒ'n stuff that they read in a book or something, you know what I mean. Just dumb ƒ'n shit and I said—"I can't take this no more. I've got to get out'"

So I said—"Boys, this is our last fuckin' gig. I'm getting out of the fuckin' business." They said—"What?" I said—"I'm not playing any more. I'm done fuckin' playing, done." So then I said—"When you get home, start looking for jobs with other fuckin' bands." I had no idea of quitting but I just said that. So when they got home, they all had to start looking for other ƒ'n jobs. That's how I broke the ƒ'n band up, without saying, "You're fired, you're fired," you know.

Of course I never retired. I kept on ƒ'n playing, but I played with this guy, that guy, hired different guys and played, and then when I got to Toronto, Donny, my buddy in Toronto said—"Why don't you make a ƒ'n album or CD or tape or something." He said—"I'll put up the ƒ'n money." So he put up the money. I went in. It took me one night. I made the ƒ'n CD and left.

I just toured around myself. I just went and booked a ƒ'n bunch of jobs and went on my own and that way, I was clear of everybody and it worked a *f* of a lot better that it did with the band. A lot better than it did with the band because you weren't listening to everybody whining and going on—"I want to go here, let's go there"—and—"I'm not making enough money"—and—"I want to bring the wife up" and you know, shit like that.

❀ ❀ ❀ ❀

Most of us normally don't like playing Sunday gigs, but at the Pumphouse Brewery in downtown Moncton, it didn't matter. As in Edmundston, the audience was mostly Francophone and they loved to party. The Pumphouse had the coolest wrap-around booths—they looked like huge barrels cut in half, the backrests of which are all covered in graffiti, everything from names of lovers to phone numbers to love notes to poems. We would have reserved a booth for the band except they were too elevated and in too high a traffic area for Dutch's wheelchair. Dutch loves to talk to people at shows, but his arthritis makes it difficult. People are often a bit drunk and they don't realize how much it hurts him when they shake his hand or give him a hug. In spite of it all, though, he never lets on how much pain he's experiencing and he greets everyone who comes up as though they are long-lost friends.

The Pumphouse has developed a good blues following in Moncton, so the audience was in tune with Dutch's music, especially his old fans, who always come out.

CHAPTER FIFTEEN

Charlottetown

Monday, November 17

I'm gonna get up in the morning
I believe I'll dust my broom
I'm gonna get up in the morning
I believe I'll dust my broom
Tell the man you've been lovin'
He can stay and have my room
I'm gonna write a letter
Tell everyone I know
I'm gonna write a letter
Tell everyone I know
If you can't find Thelma
She be in East Monroe, I know

"Dust My Broom," Elmore James

Myron's is Charlottetown's big show bar. We had a decent gig, not great, but it was a Monday—someplace on the tour had to be a Monday—and because the bar is so big, it just didn't have the same atmosphere as Grossman's or the Rainbow, or O'Costigan. Blues gigs are special when there is an intimacy with the audience.

I've gotten to know Boston's great blues duo, Paul Rishell and Annie Raines over the years. Paul mentioned one time over a drink after one of their shows at Boston's House of Blues that he was drawn to playing blues because a good performance, one where the performers and the audience connect, is an authentic spiritual experience. Modern life doesn't afford many opportunities like that any more. We are all rushing someplace and most of the time, other people are just obstacles in our way. There always seems to be someone in front of us—on the highway, in a line at the store, at the bank, on the sidewalk, at the motor vehicle department, going to communion, at the buffet. We compete with one another for jobs, clients, good deals and parking spaces. But at a blues show, everyone is part of the same group and the same experience, and a performer like Dutch can weave a spell over the audience. People allow themselves to be seduced by Dutch, to succumb to the rhythm and to his charm, and to feel as though they belong. I think that's why so many people can remember with such clarity a Dutchie show they attended many years ago.

The highlight of Charlottetown was going to The Canton Café for Chinese food. For bands visiting Charlottetown, The Canton is a necessity, no matter the time of night. After the gig, even though the Canton was not that busy, we had a hard time wheeling Dutch into the restaurant, so the subject of his affliction was on my mind as we arrived back at the Best Western MacLauchlan's to talk and have the night's last drink. He didn't mind when I asked him directly how his condition had developed.

The arthritis started years ago Dave. I noticed I got it in my little finger, eh. That finger and I couldn't *f*'n move that finger without moving the other finger with it. I was playing guitar, eh, and I said— "Holy fuck, what the *f* is this!"

It's like one day I was playing and then suddenly I wasn't, because of the *f*'n arthritis, and it's like I didn't know what to *f*'n do. Finally someone said—"Well, you sang all your *f*'n life!" I said—"Yeah, but it's not the *f*'n same." Like without the guitar, you don't have something there with you, like you know. So anyway, I just went out and sang without the guitar and it worked.

I didn't miss it at first, playing the guitar, because I was concentrating so hard on trying to sing better, you know, just get my shit going and focus on my singing. That's when I wish I could *f*'n play because I could play with Garrett.

"So who did you copy your guitar style from when you were playing?"

I always liked B. B. King, but I could never play like B. B., so I just played my own way.

I certainly played my own way in Charlottetown. I made a couple of really bad mistakes, even missing a couple of cues for solos. After a while, your mind can wander when you're playing and you end up thinking about the hockey game or the book you were reading. Dutch didn't say anything to me, but I knew he noticed. When I mentioned it to AJ he told me to relax.

"When it comes to mistakes, Dave, I don't even think about it, because a lot of times mistakes are a good thing, like something new in the song and that the band might turn around and go—'Oh jeez, I like that accent' and suddenly it's not a mistake. The thing is you don't even worry about that anymore, because especially with the blues, it's feel, like a lot of times if you start a song and the song feels like it's getting better, you don't stop it. You keep playing it and you add more to it and so you just go on. You might think it's a mistake or the band might say at the end of a set—'God, that was an awful set'—but people will come up and say—'That was the best set I ever heard you guys play.' And we're laughing our heads off. So you never really know what's good. You might think it's bad on stage because you hear everything on the stage, every mistake. But out front, the people aren't even hearing it or they might hear a mistake as an accent."

I wanted to say thanks to AJ. I knew he was trying to make me feel better. I'm not a pro like the other members of the band who have seen it all before. I still worry about my playing and I'm often insecure. It didn't help when Carter came up and pulled the rookie initiation joke on me.

"Hey Dave," he said, interrupting AJ's dissertation on mistakes. "I don't care what Dutch says. I think you sounded okay."

"Dutch said what?" I stammered. Carter laughed. He'd caught another novice with his gag.

"They don't even hear the mistake," AJ continued. "They're so involved with the music. They're there for the energy of it, the feeling of the emotion, as opposed to making sure every note is in exactly the place it should be.

"Because a lot of the songs you're playing, most of them, especially these days, are your own. Like songs that Rick Jeffery wrote or songs that Dutchie plays that he's been playing for thirty or forty years, or songs that Theresa plays that are traditional blues. Every time they're recorded, they're recorded differently by every band, so the way you're playing them, the people don't know whether you're doing it right or wrong anyway. They just like the way you're doing it, the way they're hearing it that night, that's the way they like it and it doesn't matter whether or not you're doing it right. They either like it or they don't like it and that's the way it goes."

What AJ said made sense, but knowing it to be true and feeling it in your gut when you are on stage are two different things. His words did help though.

CHAPTER SIXTEEN

The New Brunswick/ Nova Scotia Border

Tuesday, November 18

I've had my fun, if I don't get well no more
I've had my fun, if I don't get well no more.

Yeah, you know my health is failin' me now people
Oh and I am goin', goin' down slow

Yeah, tell my mother, tell her the shape I'm in,
Yeah, tell my mother, tell her the shape I'm in
Tell her to pray for me, to forgive me for my sins.

"Goin' Down Slow," J. B. Oden

Carter and I were in his truck together from Charlottetown to New Glasgow before we switched back to our normal driving arrangement. Charlie and Barry sat in the back of the Cadillac. They got to listen to AJ for a couple of hours. Carter's usually pretty quiet so it was great to have the chance to talk to him.

He talked mostly about guitar and, of course, the conversation always came back to Dutch. Carter certainly has the toughest slot in the band. I say that because Dutch was such a phenomenal guitar player. When you listen to his recordings, you can detect that it was the power of his musicianship on the guitar, even more than his vocals, that seemed to drive the band. So Carter inherited the job of setting the tone and mood for each song. Dutch likes each tune played a certain way and we all want to accomplish this. But we also have to play our own way, with our own sound. Nobody has to walk that fine line more than Carter.

Carter's distinctive mark is his tone. One chord and you know it's him. There's no mistaking his sound. He plays either his 1981 Gibson 335 or a 1972 Fender Stratocaster. His amp is a Blackface Super Reverb, or sometimes a Tweed Vibrolux with a Kendrick reverb unit.

As good a lead player as he is, Carter's real strength is his rhythm playing. Young players often only care about lead and doing solos. That's all they'll practice—trying to sound like Stevie Ray Vaughan. But the sign of a mature pro is how well they can play rhythm, and Carter is the best there is. AJ always wants Carter immediately to his right—by tradition the bass player stands to the drummer's left—because that way he can pick up the rhythm better. Sometimes a guy will sit in and AJ will complain after—even about very good players—that he couldn't pick out the beat of the shuffle being played. He would not know how to complement their groove. There is never a doubt about the groove when Carter lays it down.

"I used to see Dutchie play," Carter told me, "Dutch and Rick's band, and I said—'Oh, they'll never hire me. Like never friggin' hire me,' because I didn't play like them. They had such a big powerful sound, like a rock blues sound. I said —'Man, those guys, I never thought of playing with them. They had just a totally different style, so I never, ever thought I'd ever end up with them. But the first time I played with Dutchie would be like 1992, subbing out a gig for John Eyman with Joe Murphy and one of those gigs was New Year's Eve, with Dutch, at Your Father's Moustache and he and Joe had all these tunes together. So Joe gives me all these records—Dutch records—and said—'Learn those tunes.' So I crash-learned those tunes and got to the gig and Dutchie surprised me by not playing any of them.

"Anyway, he gets up on the stage after we play a couple of tunes and he says—'Hey Joe, hey Dog, hey Fish.' Then he looks at me and goes—'Who the hell is that?' Because we'd never met before. He came over and says—'How's it going?' So we played the night and I did all right, eh, but I didn't really play the style that he was used to, so I was kind of faking my way through it, but then after that he knew my face and I could at least go up to him and say hi to him. I thought that was pretty good. And that was the first night I met Rick. It would be 1992. Well, not the first time I saw him, but the first time I met him and that was when he had white hair. He had dyed his hair white and Dutchie laughed and they were all going—'Oh, way to go Rick, dyeing your hair white.' But it was quite a joke for Rick. He thought it was hilarious. And his mother even thought it was, I guess. She said—'Good God, what are you friggin' doing?'

"It was a cool night because Rick was there and Dutch was there and so anyway, we played that night and then I got playing with—well it was a few months later—but I got playing with Theresa Malenfant, so then I got into playing with AJ. AJ got me into Theresa's band and then Rick needed guitar players, so I got to play with him once in a while.

"One of the things was that I had a truck and I could take people to the friggin' gigs, because I don't think anybody else had a car. And then what really cinched the deal was when I bought Dutchie's station wagon. He was going—'You should buy it, you should buy it.' So I bought it and then I was in like Flynn. He'd never let me go then, which was cool. It was an Oldsmobile Custom Cruiser. It was like a tank. I drove it into the ground because it went from me to the junk yard. It lasted three years, I think. But that's how I got started playing with Dutch."

"It's kind of a cliché," I said to Carter, "but it is true that if you own the PA or a car to drive the band, you are halfway to a career in music; that and being a good guy to go on the road with. I read that even Duke Ellington would hire guys if they were good on the road."

"Playing with Dutch, yeah, that's where I got better the most—that's not even ƒ'n English—but I think I got better then. That's where I improved the most, I'd say, playing with Dutch, because he was really busy from 1995 until a couple of years ago. We were all over the place, so I learned the way Dutchie directs a band. You know, what we talk about when we're in the motel rooms, like playing with dynamics, knowing what notes to put where. It's not like Dutch sits down and tells you stuff. He never sat down and told me directly what to do. Just like night after night, if he gave you a nod or he'd give you a smile, he'd say—'Yeah,' and I'd feel like I did it right."

❖ ❖ ❖ ❖

Carter is right on about this. There's a subtlety when you're on stage with Dutch that's hard to describe to people, even to some musicians. Maybe it has to do with the order of things in the music, in spite of the background chaos. Dutch has this ability to direct people—he used to

141

be nicknamed "the director." When you're on stage with him, Dutch can just nod or turn his head or point with his thumb and the whole band reacts. We are always watching him for direction. Silently and discreetly, he conducts the full band on stage.

"And it was cool," said Carter. "Like, if Dutchie would hear you play something, whether it was a B. B. King lick, or you know, anybody, even obscure blues stuff—he likes obscure blues—he would turn around and look at me. If I would throw in a Guitar Slim lick or something—like he'd remember that. He'd remember that lick and when the guy played it, 1956 or whatever. He was a huge fan of that whole era, like Scottie Moore's playing and the beginning of rock and roll. And he knows everybody. He knows all those players. Like if you're talking about Ronnie Hawkins and the Hawks, he knows those guys, right. They were all drinking buddies and sometimes when people who don't know him hear him talk, they must think that he's lying, that he's making up stories. But I mean he showed up in Toronto and those places in early 1960 or 1962, something like that. When, you know, rock and roll was only about four or five years old.

"One thing about Dutch, and I know Dutch, is that he's always pushing you to sound like yourself. And that's what Rick always really pushed on me, was having your own sound, because he learned that from Dutchie and it's a major, major thing, having your own sound, because you're going to wish you did. There's lots of guys that don't have their own sound. I mean you don't have to insult anybody by saying they don't have their own sound; but you know, if you spend twenty years working on your instrument and you don't have your own sound, well who is going to care? That's evident with certain players, not to insult anybody. If anybody heard me say that, they'd say—'Who the fuck does he think he is?' I'm not trying to be like that, but that's what I've been taught, so that's what I believe. It's been drilled into my head by all of the blues guys here on the East Coast that have any balls whatsoever and any talent and got their own styles. I've been playing guitar since I was seventeen, so for how many years, seventeen to eighteen years and just now I'm starting to get the handle of getting my own sound, my own style. Like it takes a long time and it's from playing with guys like Dutch and Rick. They don't want to hear the same old crap. And when you look back at all of the musicians Dutchie's played with, they've all been individual players.

"Of all the guys I could mention, the guys that have put their time in and played, you know, well Dutch is the main guy. People talk about his personal life, whether you'd say he's drinking or he's whatever, that he's a party animal, that he's a nut hanging from the chandeliers and all that, but he had to have earned the utmost respect for the music he's playing or he wouldn't have done it for fifty friggin' years.

"That's the main thing: respecting the music and where it came from and educating yourself on where it came from. Tons of people don't do that. Just slap a blues name on themselves because they're playing some blues or blues influenced stuff, you know. Well, that's disrespectful, whether you like it or not, it's disrespectful for someone like me who's struggling my ass off studying this stuff all these years and you know, I work hard at it because I've been taught to work hard at it. If you don't do your homework, then how can you have respect for what you're doing.

"It's heavy, heavy, spiritual music. A lot of people when they think about Dutch, the first thing they say is—'Oh, well he drank a lot and all this stuff'—but that doesn't have anything to do with being a musician, playing blues and what you've done. And there's people who know that. He can go anywhere in Canada and pack a house. I don't know too many guys who can do that. Obviously he has been doing his homework for fifty years. So that's what matters to me. Jeez, what else can you say. You might never find your higher power or whatever you are looking for, but man, just as long as you keep trying to look for it. There's no better way to look for it than playing this music. You know, I do it all the time. Even listening to it brings me out of a depressed state and then you just can't wait to go play. There's no amount of medication that could do that, let me tell you. Not even the Wellbutrin or the Celexa."

CHAPTER SEVENTEEN

Cape Breton Island

Wednesday, November 19

Baby please don't go
Baby please don't go
Baby please don't go
Down to New Orleans
You know I love you so

You make me weep and moan
You make me weep and moan
You make me weep and moan
Don't you leave me alone
Baby please don't go

"Baby Please Don't Go," McKinley Morganfield (Muddy Waters)

This is the only soft-seater on the entire tour, meaning it's a concert in a theatre, rather than a bar gig. The Savoy Theatre in Glace Bay is one of those old restored theatres where touring artists and traveling musicals play when they come through town, where the likes of Natalie

MacMaster and the Rankin Family do regular concerts. It used to be a theatre where they showed movies under the Famous Players banner until the 1970s. Thanks to an elaborate restoration, it's a wonderful theatre that seats more than seven hundred people.

It's not like the kind of places Dutch and the guys would have often played in previous times. Bars in Sydney, Glace Bay and places like Port Hawkesbury were probably some of the roughest places they ever gigged.

Back at what used to be an old Wandlyn Motel—you can tell because of those big, pretentious pillars out front, as though the chain was modeled on the Parthenon or something—Dutch is talking about some of the places they played, nights where fights were the order of the day.

Oh we had all kinds of *f*'n fights. Like there were all kinds of fights in the bars, like one *f*'n night we were playing down in Digby at an *f*'n trailer park somewhere. Smith's Cove it was.

Yeah, we were playing and all of a sudden this guy walked up on stage and started walking away with the drums. Started walking out with the drums and I smashed him over the head with the mike stand and knocked him out. Just *f*'n, he just started walking away with the drums—*f*'n stuff like that, you know, real bad bucket of shit, you know.

Then a guy came in one night with an armload of rocks and started throwing them at the people, you know, just *f*'n nutty stuff, stuff you could never *f*'n believe, you know. You go to a dance and have rocks thrown at you. Like I mean, what the *f* is that? I seen them beat one guy up one night with one of them little kid's baseball bats, like made out of hardwood, you know, like a real bat, until they broke the *f*'n bat and the *f*'n guy was still *f*'n trying to fight back. That's how these *f*'n things were.

I don't know what it is about Digby, but we were playing there another time, and now the guy is vice president of the *f*'n legion, right, and he's loaded, and he yelled up—"Play blah, blah, blah." We were going okay and just ignoring the guy. You know those bingo tables, those long *f*'n tables that fold together. He picked one up them up and headed right for the *f*'n stage with it and knocked over the drums, microphones, guitars, amps and everything. Cleaned the *f*'n stage right off. Drums fell all over the cymbals, the drums were all over everything. And everybody in the legion was going and they all had to go. Here's the second head guy from the whole legion, and they had to take him and throw him, pin him down and they all had to carry him and throw him out of the *f*'n legion and have the cops come and take him out. And they were telling us everything was okay. This was the guy that booked us in the *f*'n legion.

One night we were playing in Kentville and a black guy was in there *f*'n around and a fight started and the cops came in and one cop was beating him with his billy, like, you know, the big long stick. Fuck, he broke the billy over his head, broke the billy now over his head so he got the, what do you call it, the leather part that was around his neck and had the *f*'n broken parts shoved right up in his neck. And he threw the cop right over his *f*'n head and got away. Now you figure that *f*'n one. I mean those guys were tough, tough, *f*'n guys. But that stuff *f*'n happened a lot. In the dance halls that happened a lot, like you'd expect three or four fights a night anyway. But when we were playing in the band, they kind of stayed away from us, like, you know.

"But you guys would sometimes also fight amongst yourselves, right?"

Oh jeez, we were in Ontario, right. And it was Ricky, of course. It was about three o'clock in the morning. We were in this restaurant and we got arguing about some *f*'n thing and I said—"Why don't you just shut up"—like that, you know. So he wouldn't stop and I reached over and I grabbed his *f*'n face and just pulled him right across the table. So anyway, outside we *f*'n went and the people in the restaurant were screaming and yelling and, you know, the whole bullshit. And it was raining like *f* out, eh. So we got outside and he punched me or some *f*'n thing in the *f*'n face and I just looked at him. So anyway, I picked him up and threw him over the fence and he came back over the fence, and I said—"Give up?" He didn't, so I shoved his *f*'n head right down in the mud and all you could see was his *f*'n two little lips and two little eyes sticking up out of the mud saying—"I give up." So I turned around and, jeez, didn't he kick me in the back with them big rock and roll boots on. Then, I beat him up.

So then I went back in the restaurant and the cops were coming and Ricky was in a phone booth trying to make a phone call, looking like James Dean or some *f*'n thing. Three o'clock in the morning, in a phone booth, raining out. You know. Then we went back to the *f*'n hotel and the next day, he came over to my room and *f*, he had scratches and scrapes all over him, and I said—"Holy fuck, you look terrible." You know, we just forgot about it the next day. So I said— "Let's go over to the restaurant to get something to eat." We went in the restaurant and the waitress went—"Ooooooh"—like that, you know. Ricky said—"Let's blow out the 401."

But we were always *f*'n fighting with one another. He'd rip a suit off me or tear the pocket off my suit or rip my shirt or, you know, just stupid shit, you know. There'd be no reason. Just stupidity. Like you know, just saying—"Go away, Ricky, you're a bother." Like when he got *f*'n drunk, like Dave, you never seen him drunk. Man, if he was here drunk, he'd fall on the TV or he'd smash the *f*'n lamp or he'd be off doing stuff like that, you know. You'd be saying—"Stop, stop, stop"— until finally you just had to pound him. That's what he was like.

One time we were playing up in the Horseshoe Valley, in *f*'n Ontario somewhere, anyway. Hidden Valley or Horseshoe Valley. Ricky and Garry Blair got the golf carts out and went all over the greens with the *f*'n things and ripped holes in it and *f*'d up the greens. Oh yeah, it was a big joke, but I was the one that used to have to take all the shit for the *f*'n jokes. No wonder I *f*'n drank. Yeah, everybody was just *f*'n around. Never anything wrong with anybody in the band. They always came to me, you know what I mean, and everybody in that *f*'n band was *f*'n crazy, you know. But they all came to me. I couldn't do anything about it. What the *f* was I supposed to do?

Ricky and Blair were the worst to try and deal with on the road. See Blair had diabetes, right and he didn't know that he did and he was all *f*'d up from that and I know what it's like having diabetes, after I knew this, like years and years later when I got diabetes and it's the *f*'n worst. It's a *f*'n killer. And Ricky was always whacked out on the junk or whatever the *f* he was doing. I don't know what he was doing. So anyway, they were the hardest to deal with, like that you know. Wade was real good but the rest of them didn't understand it was a *f*'n job. For them it wasn't a job, it was like—"Fuckin', let's go have some fun, rip this place apart." But you can't do that.

I was the one who took the *f*'n heat. One night we were playing in Campbellton. We were staying at the Wandlyn Motel, right, and I was sleeping on the second tier and I kicked Ricky about five *f*'n times and I said—"I'm going to sleep. Please let me go to sleep." So finally when he wouldn't listen, I just *f*'n threw him out the *f*'n door, shut the door and locked it tight. There was a big pane glass window right by my bed—smash! The whole *f*'n window came in all over the bed and him with it. He just pulled his *f*'n leather coat over his head and jumped through the window—jumped through the *f*'n window and there's glass all over the bed and I said—"Ricky, don't move"—because I didn't want to get all cut up, so finally I got the glass off the bed and everything and then I went downstairs and I said—"Some guy was drunk and going down the hall and slipped and fell in through my window"—and that's how I got out of it.

Why he tried to go through my window, I don't know. Just being a *f*'n asshole. I love him because he's like a *f*'n brother or some *f*'n thing. I love him. That's all it was and we were really good friends and that was it, you know. But there were a lot of weird *f*'n things that happened that I can't even think of.

Like once we were out west and we were up around Wawa and there's a lot of Indians up around there, so Ricky went in one of the gift shops right and stole a whole lot of *f*'n little buffalos and bows and arrows and stuff and put them in the *f*'n car. So then, coming back, on our way back home, we're passing by the same *f*'n place and he said—"Pull in here." So I mean, I'm driving for three *f*'n days right, so anyway, I pulled in and I'm asleep like this and I hear—boom, boom, boom!—and I'm like—"Where the fuck are we?"—and I woke up and I said—"Oh, we're at the Indian place." So anyway, he came out and said—"Quick, get out of here." I went—"Yeah"—so I take off and I asked what happened and he said—"Well, I stole a whole bunch of those little *f*'n things out of the store the other day and I think the guy seen me." So anyway, we get down the *f*'n road and he said—"Pull up this road." So it was just up in the woods, right, so he went and he took all the prices off everything and laid them down in the trunk of the car on a piece of *f*'n cloth. So now we go down the road and not two *f*'n miles—a roadblock—the cops with their *f*'n guns out and the whole deal. I said—"Oh, Jesus, I don't want to spend time in jail in *f*'n Wawa!" So we pulled over and he convinced the cops that he bought this stuff the first time by. And when there were no price tags or anything on them, no dates or anything, they couldn't do anything so they let us go. You can imagine, Mr. Lucky Ricky. He ain't so lucky now, but I mean that was him in those days. Yeah, Mr. Lucky.

He was just *f*'n nuts you know. Like for *f* sake, would you please, drinking was real bad for him because like the dope seemed to settle him down and *f*'n made him more coherent, like in order to *f*'n play, but when he got the booze, holy *f*, he was always in *f*'n trouble. Like robbing a girl's purse or stealing the door money from some bar or the *f*'n night we were playing in Ottawa and they threw a fire extinguisher out through the *f*'n window in the hotel and it landed right on the *f*'n hood of a police cruiser. And I had an interview with Margaret Trudeau the next day, so I get up, get all dressed up, go into town, have my interview, come back—all I want to do is go to *f*'n sleep.

"Oh, you're not staying here anymore, Mr. Mason." I went—"Why, what happened?" "Well, you never heard?" I went—"No, why, what happened?" Then they told me the story. I said—"All right,"—like you know. I was getting the rooms out there for free and the whole deal and then I had to go in town and pay for *f*'n rooms. Well, you know what it's like trying to put *f*'n something together and I had these assholes on the *f*'n road.

There was another time when we were all doing the pills. We were just telling band stories and stuff like that, so Ricky was out in the bedroom and he's got James Brown playing. He had a tape recorder and the tape recorder had James Brown playing, whatever the tune was, ten

times, over and over, going and going. And we were out in the other room drinking and we were playing something else, like country music or something. Ricky came running out and said—"Turn that fuckin' music down." We went—"You're playing that fuckin' James Brown thing over and over and over." So doesn't he take a kick at AJ.

"No," said AJ. "First he put a brick in the door. I tried to close the door, so he opened the door and put a brick in the door. So then I'm going, would you *f* off. So I came back in, kicked the brick away and pulled the door closed. Then he'd sneak out, he'd wait for us to sit down and you would hear the door open and the brick going at the door again and James Brown came back on again. So I, you know, after about four or five times of this, I'm getting *f*'d because I'm on the pills. I go running into the room and I said—'Turn that shit off.' So I grabbed the cassette deck and he grabs me, starts kicking at me and all that so I ended up jumping on top of him, started beating the hell out of him and Dale and Dutchie come in there, pulling me off. I got Ricky then on the floor and I'm trying to wreck his tape deck. For some reason we hit the record button on his thing and you could hear the fight recorded over his James Brown tune. You could hear all this stuff like on Seinfeld, eh. You hear all this noise in the middle of James Brown."

It was so *f*'n funny because he threw Ricky right up in the *f*'n air and Ricky turned right around and landed on his head.

"And here I am about 5'5" and Ricky is about 6'2" or 6'3", something like that. That was the first time I ever had a fight with Ricky. But that was—oh my god—he was there to irritate us. He knew we were all on pills. He always tried to find a way.

"Like this time we're up in Campbellton. Ricky and Dale were doing their pills, so they ran out and Ricky said—'Dale, you got to drive me up to the hospital—we got to get more pills.' So Dale said—'Okay, let's go.' We go out and get this car that Dutchie just bought, this Oldsmobile. So they get in the car, they go up to the hospital and get their pills. Now Dale is all stoned. He falls asleep and he's in the back seat of the car while Ricky is in the hospital getting pills and when he comes out, Ricky gets in the driver's seat. He doesn't have a license. He comes back down from the hospital and smashes into this guy's car, this old fellow and he's also driving a brand new Oldsmobile—a brand new car. Ricky goes right through the stop sign, smashes into him. Now the first thing that happens, he wakes Dale up and tells Dale to get in the driver's seat because Ricky doesn't have a license.

"Dale is just waking up with these pills, right. And he's going—'What the fuck just happened?' The cars are in the middle of the road before the cops got there and this old fellow is too old, you know. It takes him a while to get out so they switch drivers. So Ricky said—'Your name is Ricky Jeffery and I'm Dale White.' So the cop gets there and in the meantime, Dale is still going, like baffled—'What the fuck happened?' So the cop gets there and says—'Okay, now what happened?' Ricky is going—'Well this Rick Jeffery here was driving the car and he just got in the accident.' Dale goes—'Wait a sec.' The cop said—'what's your name?' And Dale said—'Oh, I'm Rick Jeffery' and then Ricky goes—'Yeah, and I'm Dale White.'

"So this goes on and the cop says—'what was your name again?' Dale looked over at Ricky and says—'Rick, what was my name again? What was my name?' Rick goes—'It's Rick.' 'No,' says Dale, 'Rick, what's *my* name?' And Ricky said—'I'm not Rick, you're Rick. I'm Dale.' Dale then says—'What's wrong with you. You're Rick.' And the cop is going—

'What the fuck?' So for some reason, they let them go back to the house we were at. In the meantime they're in the house making all these *f*'n stories up because they got to wait until the next day because the cop has got to get this all together and everything. That night they're back in the room there and they're sitting there scamming."

No you missed the whole *f*'n story, AJ. I'm in the hotel room and it's like nine in the morning and the phone rings. I pick up the phone and they say—"Is this Mr. Mason?" I said—"Yeah." They said—"Do you own such and such automobile?" I said—"Yeah." They said—"Well, it's been in an accident." I went—"Well I haven't been driving it." Well they said—"It's been all smashed up. Rick Jeffery smashed the car up." But I get back and Dale is Rick, you know what I mean. And the car is all smashed to *f* in the front, like that you know. And they're trying to scam off some kind of a deal where they didn't do any *f*'n thing.

"So Al, 'Silk,' our manager, is out there at the car with coat hangers and everything. He's trying to get the muffler fixed cause it's hanging on the ground. He's trying to tape up the bumper—he's got duct tape, he's got coat hangers—just so he can go back to Halifax. It was the stupidest *f*'n thing. They kept calling you, the cops, eh Dutch, but you never got charged, did you?"

No. It never happened, no.

"And this car was written off," says AJ. "A brand new Oldsmobile Fifth Avenue. He never got charged for it. They got off. Now how the *f* they ever got off, I don't know."

I think that was the *f*'n time I said—"That's it, no more fuckin' band, no more nothing." I said—"I'm going home boys. I can't take it no more. You got me fuckin' crazy." I mean we're talking about the same guy—Dale—who we found in a closet one time. Dale was supposed to be on a diet. Dale said—"I'm going on a diet. That's it." We said—"Well, that's good Dale." So anyway, he was on the diet right. So one night I came back and there was nobody in the room, but I said—"I smell *f*'n chicken, Kentucky Fried Chicken," like that. I looked all around, opened up the *f*'n closet and there's Dale in the closet with these blue underwear on, not a stitch of clothes on. With a box of *f*'n Kentucky Fried Chicken, eating it. "I just got to have a drink and eat a little bit of this chicken. I was almost starved to death," he said. He went right into it like he was *f*'n nuts. No lights or anything, the closet closed. He was sitting in the closet with a whole bucket of chicken in his blue underwear, those blue underwear with the white stripes, sitting there with a bucket of chicken between his legs, like that, you know. You could hear the noise. There he was, sitting there, eating the whole bucket of chicken and on a diet.

❉ ❉ ❉ ❉

Now imagine that the same guy sitting in that closet eating KFC in the dark told me once that he used to work in an office job with the Department of National Defence and was working his way toward a pension. At age twenty-eight or twenty-nine, he decided on music as a way of life. And as crazy as he and Ricky would be at times, Dale gave me a clear perspective on life one night when we chatted.

"Wealth comes in many, many forms," he told me, waxing philosophically. "And when you're sitting on the rocking chair, hopefully in your eighties, hopefully you live that long, you need to accumulate the real wealth, in your mind, heart and soul."

This from a guy who was jamming with Huey Lewis in St. John's, Newfoundland, and who kept a Cooper bottle, the kind of water bottle that hockey players use, half filled with one-hundred-proof vodka and orange juice, sitting on the top of his amp. He didn't want to take his hands off the bass while he was playing, so he would straddle over to the bottle on the top of the amp, and take a drink without missing a note.

❀ ❀ ❀ ❀

See what happened with Ricky, you know if you're in a band or some f'n thing and you're leaving the band, you would go to the band guy and say—"Look, I'm quitting in a couple of weeks," like that, you know, and "I'll try to find you a harp player or somebody," like that. He tells me the night before a gig that he quits. The night before a gig he quit the f'n band. He just told me—"I can't go to Fredericton." I said—"You can't go to Fredericton. Why, what's wrong?" He said— "Well I got my own band together." I said—"Ricky, you can't organize a circle jerk. What are you talking about putting a band together. You just can't put nothing together." And of course, he didn't.

"Dutch," I said, "I know how proud you are of what Ricky actually did accomplish after setting out on his own. You told me that yourself many times. Just the way Muddy Waters used to talk about all the guys who left his band and went on to careers as frontmen."

AJ added: "Well, actually about six months later, he did end up with that f'n blues band. What were they called? Blues Blast?"

The Halifax Explosion. I said to Rick, "All the best." He tells me the night that we're supposed to leave to go to *f*'n Fredericton. Imagine.

"Ricky told me one time something about a gig you were playing in Toronto or Ottawa or maybe Kingston, and he got hooked up with the motorcycle gang, the Vagabonds?"

And they beat him up. What happened was they came up to *f*'n me, the guys, the Vagabonds and they said—"Do you want to come down to the club house, Dutch, and have a few drinks or something after you're done playing?" I said—"No guys, I'm so *f*'n tired, I just want to go back to the hotel and go to *f*'n sleep." I just didn't want to get down to the *f*'n club house with them. So anyway, I really didn't want to go there because I knew if Ricky was going, I'd be in trouble. So anyway, away he *f*'n went.

Jeez, about eight o'clock in the morning, I heard this—crash, bang, smash—and I looked out and there was Ricky laying out in front of the door of this *f*'n hotel, all beaten to *f*. So I just dragged him inside, threw him in the *f*'n bed and the next day, I went in about noon and the *f*'n blood was just stuck right to him. I had to peel the bed sheets off his *f*'n face, like that, and the pillow and everything. He said they were shooting pool at the Vagabond place and Ricky said—"I hear they call you guys the 'Fag'-abonds." And the guy came over and the Sergeant-at-arms, like the guy in charge, said—"Just leave him alone. He is with Dutch's band." Didn't Ricky turn around and say to the Sergeant-at-Arms—"You stay out of this, it's none of your *f*'n business." The Sergeant-at-Arms just said—"He has to play harp for Dutch, so leave his *f*'n mouth alone." That was it. They beat the shit out of him and drove him back to the *f*'n place. What a *f*'n asshole.

We played for the Hell's Angels. I think they were just changing into Hell's Angels then and we knew all those guys really well too, you know, so that was kind of good in a way, you know. We got to know a lot of bikers, but they'd kind of scare away the other people if they had their collars on. It didn't make any ƒ'n difference to me. They could come bare naked, it wouldn't make any ƒ'n difference. But it hurt the crowds.

Anyway, I didn't care. I liked most of them. I liked all of them really. Anyway that was ƒ'n part of our life.

"Tell me about the hairdresser thing," I said. "Ricky told me part of it one time but to tell you the truth, I couldn't piece together what he was saying."

We were in Montreal, staying at the Shearborne. Now I'm in my ƒ'n room, like that, sitting there having a drink, right. Ricky walks in and he goes—"That fuckin' Aerosmith, fuckin' no good cocksuckers." I said—"Who's Aerosmith?" I didn't know what the ƒ Aerosmith was. "Who the fuck is Aerosmith?" "Oh, it's a fuckin' rock and roll band. They bought every bit of fuckin' dope down to Maine."

That's what he was mad at. So I said—"Well, that's too fuckin' bad,"—and I got up and I said—"Well, I'm going down to this fuckin' barbershop around the corner here because I got to get a fuckin' shave. I don't dare trust myself with a razor."

So I go down around the ƒ'n corner and he is shaving me right, and he's shaving me, but he's sweating and the sweat is dropping on my face and he's wiping it off. Ricky comes over and whispers in my ear—"That guy is fuckin' stoned man. Ask him where he got his dope because his eyes are pinned and he's sweating." And I said—"Holy fuck, here we fuckin' go." So anyway, I said to the ƒ'n guy, I said—"Where can a guy get ƒ'n hooked up anyway." He said—"What do you mean, man?" I said—"You know, like some type of heroin or something, any fuckin' thing, whatever the fuck it was." "Well" he said, and then the next thing I know Ricky is shaving me and it's like I'd like to get the ƒ out of here. Anyway, Ricky talked the ƒ'n guy into coming with us on the road. I had a hairdresser on the road with us for four months. Can you imagine? But that was some of the ƒ'n things Ricky would pull.

"Ricky told me one time about a gig you guys were supposed to play in North Dakota but never made it."

No. I didn't want to go. It was Ricky who wanted to go down to some ƒ'n place in Montana to cut across, you know, and I said they won't let us in there. I said—"We all got ƒ'n records, they're not going to let us across and you got a record that ƒ'n long they won't even let you close to the ƒ'n border." So we went there anyway. Why I went I'll never know.

They're in the ƒ'n office, the guys that lead you, the border guards, they're all in there laughing. And I'm looking like this, and I'm going—"Oh, we're ƒ'd!" So anyway Ricky said they came out and they emptied his bag out and he's got needles and the ƒ'n thing, this and that, and I'm standing there and they said—"We can't let you guys across the ƒ'n border like that, you know. You all got ƒ'n records. You got to turn around and go back." Ricky says—"Ha! Try and come up to Calgary some time." I said—"Gee, that really upset them, Rick." You know, like ƒ, just an idiot.

But he'd talk me into this ƒ'n bullshit and I'd go along with it just so he'd shut up. I ƒ'n hated it. Blair was the same way you know. He was no ƒ'n angel either, you know. He'd get all drunked up, like when he was in jail in Saskatoon. We had to go down and drag him out of there. He had no *f*'n clothes on in the cell, with puke all over and every *f*'n thing and his wife Mary goes around saying her husband holds the band together. I told someone the next day—"Yeah, he really holds the *f*'n band together."

And there was another *f*'n border story. We were in St. Stephen. So I had a big *f*'n Mercury. I think it was bigger than the Caddie. A big *f*'n thing. So anyway, every afternoon, we would get Garry Blair—AJ wasn't with us then—Blair was with us and there would be me and Blair and Ricky and Dale. And we'd go across the *f*'n border and the guy would say—"Where are you going?" "Just over the Calais Inn to have a couple of drinks and we'll be back." "Okay fellows, go ahead," they said. And we'd go over. So we'd get ten rolls of *f*'n quarters and put the money in the jukebox and play "Old Dogs And Countrymen" and just play that constantly and have the guy turn it up full blast and drive everybody out of the place and we would be loaded drunk, drinking *f*'n wild turkey and that and *f*'n beer and then we'd come back across the border. This went on all *f*'n week and we would see a band over there called the Bill Jenick Blues Band. What a *f*'n band. They were from Boston but somehow they wound up down there. Anyway, what a great band they were.

Anyway, we were coming back across the border, so I just pulled up at an intersection, loaded *f*'n drunk, eh, and just stopped. The car was so long, I had to nose it out a little bit. I was out maybe a foot, maybe two feet. Didn't this guy come along, heading right for my *f*'n car. He was bent down in the seat, like you couldn't see his head. And I went like—"What the *f*?" So here I am and I couldn't get the thing in reverse to back it up. He hit the front end of my car, right. The *f*'n door fell right off his *f*'n car and here was a little baby laying on the *f*'n seat.

He was bent down trying to fix the baby a bottle or something and ran right into me and the car stopped right in front of the police station. That's where his car stopped. So I just ƒ'n said—"I got to go"—and they said—"Go ahead." He said it was his fault. I said—"Jeez, is the baby okay?" It didn't even put a dent in the bumper but his ƒ'n door fell right off and he had a little baby there.

CHAPTER EIGHTEEN

Truro

Friday, November 21

You are playing with my mind woman;
you are always accusin' me of doin' wrong
You are playing with my mind woman;
you are always accusin' me of doin' wrong
I see the lights are on baby, but there ain't nobody home
Now here come my mother-in-law, she drive by here every day
Now here come my mother-in-law, she drive by here every day
Ever since we been married, she's been by here every day

"Lights Are On But Nobody's Home," Gary Collins

I'd had it in my head for weeks that in Truro we were playing the Ponderosa Restaurant, one of the chain of restaurants. Truro has one, sure enough. You can see it from the main highway leading to Halifax. It was puzzling, but everyone kept saying we're playing the Ponderosa. So I'd figured, well in Truro, the town being what it is, maybe they make the best of it and convert the restaurant into a bar at night. I sure can be a knob at times. AJ looked at me like I was an idiot when I asked him why we were driving past the bar.

"What are you talking about Dave," he asked. Then laughing, he said:

"Oh, I get it. Good joke Dave. You had me going there."

"Yeah," I said, pretending that I'd been pulling his leg. "Good joke eh?" Then I added: "Hey Dutch, did you ever hear about the time that AJ, Carter and I were playing at Melvin's in Saint John. We were with Theresa and it was a slow night. Between sets Carter said—'Okay guys, let me buy you a drink. I can't drink anymore, but at least let me buy you a shooter'—I got a Fireball, that stuff you drink sometimes. AJ asked what it tasted like and I said—'Chicken bones.' 'Chicken bones?'—he asked—'Who the f would drink something that tasted like chicken bones?' I had no idea what he was going on about, but he kept looking horrified. Finally, Carter clued in—'AJ, you jerk. Not chicken soup bones. Chicken bones. The candies they serve at Christmas.' 'Oh' is all AJ could say."

The Ponderosa Tavern is way over on the far reaches of Main Street, on the cusp of Bible Hill. It was around three in the afternoon when we pulled the El Dorado into the parking lot of "The Pond," as it's affectionately known locally. It looks modern enough on the outside, with the kind of bland, beige aluminum or vinyl siding that one sees in North York or Scarborough. It's in a quasi-industrial part of town, back on the railway tracks and neighboring such other businesses as MacKenzie's Auto Mart, Chantilly's Diner and the Damascus Restaurant.

"Any good, Dutch, the Damascus pizza?" I inquired.

Dave, at two or three in the morning, pizza's f'n pizza.

Inside, the place was long and spacious. "Huge" would be a more apt description, with tables on a raised landing to the left, a cordoned-off lottery terminal arcade to the right, a long stand-up bar, a pool table, a raised DJ booth and the biggest dance floor I'd seen in years. Behind the

bar there were six two-foot-square, stainless steel fridge doors mounted to the wall, concealing copious amounts of bottled beer. The doors
were covered in a burgundy red vinyl, a treatment I'd never seen before.
They reminded me for some reason of the upholstered furniture you
might see in a brothel. The raised landing to the left felt like part of the
main room, but a small plastic red and white sign which read: "Dining
Room," which seemed a bit of an exaggeration. But then it occurred to
me that most everything at "The Pond" was a bit tongue-in-cheek.

There was a wall of hockey, baseball, water polo and dart team
photos and hockey sticks mounted along the wall to the left, but to
the right, just as there should be, was a four-by-seven-foot rendering
of the Cartwrights—Little Joe, Hoss, Pa and that other brother most
people, including me, can't name—standing gloriously in front of
the Ponderosa house. It was a painting by someone named Perley
MacLellan.

After we loaded in and set up, I sat at a table and gleaned a Xerox
copy of the menu, which is fronted with a string of "Rules and
Regulations." Some of the points raised were rules, others read like
random thoughts:

All Meals available with small Caesar Salad or Garden Salad for $2.50
We are not a restaurant, but a way of life.
Not responsible for lost or stolen articles, bad punctuation or mis-
spelled words.
If you do not like the way I do things—buy me out.
No chewing gum under the tables—only staff allowed.
If you are looking for linen—wrong place.
We promise friendly and courteous service at reasonable prices and for
any reason we fail to the live up to this promise, Don't Tell Anyone!!!

As I read it, I kept going back to regulation number five; I couldn't help but wonder if only the staff are allowed under the tables or if only the staff are allowed to place chewing gum under the tables. I've been correcting the grammar in students' papers for too long. My father used to do that and I hated it. "Can I go out?" I would ask. "Not 'Can I,'" he would say, "May I go out." "Yeah, yeah, but can I *f*'n go out," I would think. So I would ask properly and then he would say no.

Dutch, AJ and the boys have all been here, all played here before over the years. A fifty-ish waiter named John, a friendly guy with a mid-life build, told me "The Pond" used to be a biker bar. "It was a tough place during its day," he says.

The place was built in 1956 by Harold Bates, who owned Hub Beverages. But on July 17, 1963, the *Bible Hill Free Press* proclaimed "Bible Hill Is Wet," the headline summing up the result of a plebiscite held and passed the previous year in Central Colchester County supporting the opening of taverns. Five days later, "The Pond" opened for the purpose of selling bottled and draught beer; Bates apparently sold the beverage business that same year.

I decided that even though it was still before dinner, I was going to have a drink which is something I rarely do. Carter noticed and began to tease me over it.

"Look guys, Dave's becoming a drunk just like the rest of us. What's Sue going to say about this?"

The waiter John—John Owen—was wonderfully talkative. Not overly familiar, just talkative. It was clear he was excited about Dutch's gig.

"Like I said, this was always a biker's place, but to tell you how much things have changed, a lot of those same guys ride up now in their forty thousand dollar machines and expensive leather. They come in and instead of ordering a steak and a pitcher of draught and looking for a fight, they ask what red wines we have and order a spinach salad."

John told me they actually had a reunion last year for all the regulars around fifty years old who had come to "The Pond" for their first underage drink, and who were barred for fighting when the place was definitely a rocker bar.

"Whenever, it doesn't matter when it is, when Dutch is playing here, it's packed." He thinks the last time was a benefit for a local lad who was losing his eyesight. John waxed on, almost sentimentally, about what it's like when Dutch plays the room.

"He touches everybody. It's like he has this deep respect for his audience. It's the way he talks to them, like he has this respect for them. Not like a lot of guys today who get up and kind of go on like they're a bit smart-assed or cocky. Dutch talks to his audience."

With a great hometown crowd for Dutch, the Truro gig went really well. Describing Dutch afterward, the bar's owner, John Cavanagh said "He is phenomenal. He can lay down ten songs or two songs and the crowd is just as happy. He brings out the best in people and he brings out a lot of people that don't even come out here anymore."

CHAPTER NINETEEN

Halifax

Saturday, November 22

I may be gettin' old, but I got young fashioned ways
You know I'm gonna love a good woman the rest of my natural days
A young horse is fast, but an old horse knows what's goin' on
A young horse wins the race, but an old horse lasts so long.

"Young Fashioned Ways," Willie Dixon

By Halifax, everyone was tired and beginning to get cranky with each other—with inanimate objects even—as we struggled one more time to haul sixty-pound amps out of the truck and carry them upstairs and through narrow doors. I can't remember how many times I've scraped the same knuckles trying to maneuver my Super through a doorway.

We were energized, though, when we arrived at Bearly's. We've all played there so many times that we know the staff, many of the regulars and every square inch of the stage, bar and kitchen.

"Mimi, how are you doin'?" said AJ, who can almost call the bar home. Mimi even takes phone messages for him there.

"You guys are early tonight," he said. "Looks like it should be a good crowd."

Mimi doesn't have to ask what drinks we want. He just serves them up—one of the advantages of hanging around bars for a living. Dutch is taken to the kitchen in the back. He has his spot up against the freezers. There, he's relatively protected from the mob of fans who stream in to say "Hello." They all get their turn, but only a few at a time, which suits Dutch better. He can also smoke back there at will. Halifax, like many other cities, has passed by-laws to reduce smoking in bars and restaurants. Dutch needs a place to smoke because going without a cigarette is not an option.

By default, Bearly's is more or less home base now for all of us. It's a small, multi-level place at the far end of Barrington Street. There's are a dozen or so tables sprinkled around the main floor, with a small corner stage situated opposite a modest bar accompanied by a half dozen or more wooden stools. You can climb a handful of stairs to a second level where the conversation's easier because the music is buffered by a wall of windows.

At Bearly's, urgings scrawled across small pieces of Bristol board rest against window panes facing the street. The inside is a sea of blackboards hawking drink specials, food specials, lists of who's playing when and invitations for patrons to join in on the regular Sunday night jam, which usually begins around nine. I've been at the jam and heard the MC for the evening say "this is the Romper Room of the blues," where anyone can show up and learn the feel of the blues. This is also where I first heard a guy talk about his harp as being "four and three-quarter inches of pure music."

Bearly's has taped blues music playing perpetually in the background. It's never overbearing—it's just always on. When you're playing there, the wood floor easily fills with dancers. Between sets, AJ and I wheeled Dutch into the kitchen, where even though it's still operating and food was still being prepared, we hung out. As the gig finished, it became clear that Dutch is still an icon. No matter who else was on stage that night—it didn't matter. Dutch was the reason everyone was there.

As always happens when we play at Bearly's, we got a lot of jammers showing up. Bearly's is the hang-out for blues musicians in Halifax. They drift in after their own gigs are done. The third set, from one to two in the morning, is a constant rotation of blues players. For this gig, Danny Sutherland and Dale "Soupbone" White sat in on bass. Mark Green played the guitar for a few tunes and sang one of Ricky's songs. Mark helped organize the big benefit last year for Ricky and he is particularly respectful of the blues tradition and the older generation of players who established the blues scene in the Maritimes. He sang "It Ain't Easy Being Sleazy" as a tribute to Ricky.

Finally, Garrett Mason got up to sing and play. Dutch's whole demeanor changed. Through all his pain, this is what he lives for.

Play it like f'n Albert Collins, he said to Garrett as we started "The Moon Is Full."

In developing his own sound, Garrett has already mastered, in his early twenties, the styles of the great guitar players. Like Carter, he too is doing his homework, showing respect for the music by learning its past. Garrett has become an excellent singer and songwriter, belying his age with a maturity of performance one rarely sees. When he first started out he was hesitant to sing, but Dutch always pushed him. He would say—*You've go to f'n sing or you will always be just a sideman and the money's in being the f'n leader.*

If you sing, the band is yours. You book the gigs, you hire the other players and you make better money. Those are just the facts.

CHAPTER TWENTY

Dutch's Apartment, Truro

Sunday, November 23

I got a sweet little angel, I love the way she spread her wings
Yes, I got a sweet little angel, I love the way she spread her wings
Yes, when she spread her wings around me, I get joy in everything

You know I asked my baby for a nickel, and she gave me a twenty dollar bill
Oh, yes, I asked my baby for a nickel, and she gave me a twenty dollar bill
Whoa, you know I asked her for a little drink of liquor,
And she gave me a whiskey still

Ah, yes, asked my baby to quit me, well, I do believe I will die
Yes, I asked my baby to quit me, well, I do believe I will die
'Cause, if you don't love me little angel,
please tell me the reason why.

"Sweet Little Angel," B. B. King/Jules Taub

Dutch was settled onto his bed and I think happy with the way the tour went; and he was happy to be back in his apartment, as small as it is. I said something about Garrett from the night before that struck a chord with him.

"You know it was incredible seeing Garrett up there on stage last night. He reminded me of how you looked in those old photos of you that Pam showed me."

Yeah, well go look at that picture over there, one that Pam loaned me, of me for *f*'s sake. It's of me and she's loaned it to me. She says that in it, I look like Garrett.

The picture of Dutch, circa 1950s, shows a lanky guy a la Elvis or Jerry Lee Lewis, with that early rock and roll look. And man, in those old black and whites, does he ever look like Garrett does today.

"That's really funny, Dutch, that Pam had to lend you this photo of you, because you probably don't have any of yourself around, eh?"

I don't think so, Dave. I think she's got 'em all, pictures of me and all the bands over the years.

❊ ❊ ❊ ❊

Pam and Dutch were married on November 26, 1981. At first they were going to get married in August of the previous year, then it was the next Valentine's Day, then July, then in the Gaspé Peninsula. It finally happened in their apartment in Halifax with an ex-Supreme Court judge who, almost prophetically, had arthritis so bad he had to sit down the whole time he was performing the ceremony.

I've talked before to Dutch's ex-wife Pam. They're not together, but she is happy to talk about him. She brings up things about Dutch, like his desire to be a tap dancer—things that the public and even his musician friends never see. She knew the side of him that was athletic, that he played ball and hockey. She knows that Kenny Clattenburg was the only friend Dutch had who he could truly confide in. She can talk about Dutch's use of the "f" word, recognizing that it's just part of the English language to him, but she knows also that he knows his place; meeting an elderly person or someone in the business world, he's able to catch himself and be polite.

Pam is a lovely person—polite and friendly, attractive and well spoken. Her apartment is as neat and tastefully decorated as Dutch's is ramshackle and disheveled. She is the kind of person whose warmth and honesty are immediately apparent. I can see why Dutch survived as well as he did for so many years with his crazy playing schedule and increasingly debilitating arthritis. And I can see why Garrett is the young man that he is. Pam and Dutch share a deep pride in their son, who will be the next great blues player in Canada, as much for who he is as for how well he sings and plays.

❊ ❊ ❊ ❊

Dutch tells stories about his family but never about what is inside him. He rarely reveals how he feels. Sometimes it comes through to the perceptive listener, but he is a private person. Norman Mason, husband and father, is an introvert, close to the vest with what's going on inside. Dutch the public performer is much more gregarious and shockingly unconcerned about how he appears to others. I wonder how the naked man lying on the bed can tell me about his past drinking excesses, and yet be almost too shy to tell me that he can't bring himself to go to funerals, even of close friends, because they make him cry and he doesn't like to make a scene in public.

Dutch, like many of us, hides from public view the kinds of memories that bring out tears and feelings that are too hard and too painful to look at. Everyone has their mistakes and moments of guilt, their longing for forgiveness and salvation. In this, he is not unique.

CHAPTER TWENTY-ONE

Fredericton

Sunday, November 23

Some of ya ain't been south ????
I'm gonna tell ya what it's all about
There used to be a weed grown in the field
Some people call it Polk Salad
I used to know a girl up on the hill
Every night around supper time, she would come around
And cook up a mess of it
And what she couldn't cook, she would put in a pipe and smoke it
Polk Salad Annie

"Polk Salad Annie," Tony Joe White

It was good to finally be home. No more endless loading and unloading gear. No more getting to bed at five or six in the morning. No more living in a car and sleeping in a strange bed. No more eating at the cheapest place to cut down on expenses. And no more breathing in secondhand cigarette smoke. Some people thrive on the road. Dutch, who was once the ultimate road warrior, is certainly worn out now that he is getting older and his health is not good. The pain from the arthritis takes a toll. AJ, though, is in his element on the road. He loves everything about it, especially hanging out with Dutch and the guys, the partying, and the excitement of playing and feeling free and important. I am glad to have undertaken the experiment, but like Carter, I just really want to be back home.

As soon as I walked through the door, I could tell that something was wrong. The hug I got was more sympathy than passion and after three weeks away that was not what I had hoped for.

"Dan called," Sue said, "It's about Rick. You better call him back right away." We all knew that Rick was not doing well. It was almost exactly a year since he had had a double lung transplant. We'd all been in touch with him in Toronto, where he'd gone for the surgery, and at first he seemed to be doing well. He was flirting with the nurses and entertaining them with stories of being on the road with the Dutch Mason Blues Band. And Ricky had plenty of stories. No one was crazier in a wild bunch of guys than Rick Jeffery had been before he quit drugs and cleaned himself up. The scar on his face spoke of it. Rick had stopped taking heroin and had quit drinking but found it much harder to quit smoking. It always reminded me of Al Capone, who ran the biggest organized crime syndicate and yet ended up in jail for tax evasion. Ricky beat every kind of addiction in Christendom and yet was lying in hospital because he could not give up cigarettes. Even when his emphysema was really bad and he could hardly walk, he still always had a chew of tobacco in his mouth. It was as though he had used up all of his will power getting off drugs and had nothing left.

I knew that the news about Rick was not going to be good. I prepared myself for it. Rick had been failing, developing an infection in his lungs, and because of his weakened state and the anti-rejection drugs, he was not fighting it off. After I returned the call to Dan, I spoke to Carter who was very close to Rick and who, like Rick, lived in Halifax. He had been to see him and had a chance to say his goodbyes. I called the hospital that night and spoke to Rick's daughter, Christine.

"Dad's failing, and he is now too weak to talk on the phone," she said. She asked if there was a message I wanted to leave.

"Just give his hand a squeeze and tell him that he is in my thoughts and that I love him."

As I hung up the phone, a wave of memories came flooding over me.

Sue and I had a special affection for Rick. When he was in Fredericton playing we would invite him for dinner and he would talk to Sue about his health and his struggle to get himself better. He looked forward to the lung transplant as though it was his promised land. Once he got there, he thought, he would get his breath and his strength back. The last time he was over at our place he announced that he had good news.

"Great Ricky. You deserve some luck going your way for a change," I said. "What's the news?"

"The doctors said that I only have two years to live." He said it with an air of satisfaction and triumph that only Rick could manage in that circumstance. Sue simply sat there, quite unable to find a suitable pleasantry with which to respond.

"Great stuff Rick," I managed, trying to be upbeat.

"That is the fucking mess I'm in," he said. "Me, Johnny Shitty-end-of-the-stick. The best I can hope for is to look like I'm dying soon so that I can get on the list for a transplant. Maybe now they will try to fix me. I don't want to be morose. I had an uncle once who all he did when he came over was talk about his illness and how crummy he felt. I never liked it when he came to visit and I always tried to tell myself not to be like that. Now here I am in your kitchen and all I have talked about are my lungs. I don't want to be just some fucking disease. I just want to get well enough to be with my son Joe and to play the harp one more time like I used to. I have written all these songs and I have so many licks in my head and I can't get them out because I can't fucking breathe."

Rick was certainly the most unusual person I have ever met. He was at once charming and hard, sensitive and extraordinarily vulgar, thoughtful and crooked. Dutch was the Prime Minister of the Blues and Rick was the Finance Minister. And no one meant that as a compliment. He fought with his band mates over money so often and so vociferously that it became a kind of joke. He knew every way imaginable to get an extra five dollars for himself out of a gig. He was also unnervingly unselfconscious about his behavior when taking drugs. Like the time he had to go to the bathroom during a set and he didn't want to get Dutch mad at him by leaving while the band was playing. In his drunken state, he thought that he could pee up against the half wall that separated the stage from the dance floor. He thought no one would notice if he just stood up close to the wall and relieved himself. As he began to urinate he noticed that the people in front who were dancing started to jump back and shout in disgust. Rick realized that what he thought was a half wall was nothing more than a railing and that he had soaked a group of dancers. Telling this story caused him no real embarrassment, which I found hard to imagine at first. Only after I got to know Rick was I able to intuit how someone could be so uncouth and yet so contemplative.

It took much cajoling to get him to come to the house for dinner the first time. His hesitancy stemmed from his recognition that a lifetime spent on the road, living without a schedule or a place that is yours or a family or the responsibility to look after yourself, had put him out of synch with respectable society. He was worried that he would not act properly around Sue. Once we convinced him that he really was welcome he relaxed and enjoyed his visits with us. He did, though, always use his Sunday best manners around Sue, and he often told me how much her friendship meant to him.

We all hoped that the new lungs Rick got would bring him the redemption that he had so longed for. He knew that he had made mistakes and that they had cost him his wife and had eaten away at his extraordinary harp skills, and all he wanted was a chance to start over and to make good on what he had done wrong. He was not morose about what drugs had cost him any more than he was embarrassed about his past behaviour. They were facts and he accepted them even if he did not feel especially proud of them. His songs spoke of his struggles in macabre and surprisingly funny and candid ways. Their honesty and insight and humor reveal Ricky's paradoxical character.

In "Skin Off My Tattoos" he wrote about his own impending death, pleading with the Grim Reaper. The song ends with a plaintive "Adios, Amigos," expressing the likelihood that Death would not let him redeem himself. In "It Ain't Easy Being Sleazy," he told of how his days as a drug addict and his fascination with pimps and gangsters had cost him his marriage.

All Rick ever wanted was to be Dutch's harmonica player. He had tried school, enrolling in Acadia University, where his uncle was a well-known mathematician. His academic career ended early, though, when instead of answering the questions on an English exam he wrote of his love for the harp. His professor called him in and asked him if he was any good at the blues and after Rick responded in the affirmative she told him that perhaps that is where he should pursue his fortune. He would never become a professor, but not because he wasn't smart or creative. Ricky's song lyrics were full of clever observations and wry metaphors. "My Baby is a Psychopath" is a funny song. It goes:

Well Sunday morning you can find her in church
With all the devils waiting in the lurch
I like to hear her when she's singing these hymns
The next full moon will have her howlin' agin.

My Baby is a psychopath
Ooh I don't know if I should cry or laugh
I don't know if I should come or go
I can't win, I can't place, I can't show.

Marie Antoinette said "let them eat cake"
And Louis knew that her mind was baked
Nero fiddled while he burnt down Rome
His lights were on but no one was home

My baby is a psychopath
Ooh I don't know if I should cry or laugh
I don't know if I should come or go
I can't win, I can't place, I can't show.

Rick Jeffery

When he left university, Rick was already majoring in heroin and life on the road with Dutch was more appealing—he could hear the call of the wild and it would not let him go. Rick's brother Jack was also in Dutch's band. Being Dutch's harp player meant that whatever self doubts he might have had, and he had many, and whatever anxieties he might have labored under, Rick could always walk into a room with a strut knowing that he had achieved the pinnacle in the blues world. He played with the Prime Minister of the Blues.

After Dutch broke the band up Rick formed his own band, "The Rick Jeffery Blues Blast." He still played most of Dutch's gigs, opening up each set with a few of his own songs and directing the band on the stage. Rick had notable accomplishments on his own though, once he stepped out from Dutch's shadow. He put out two CDs and wrote many songs. He was most proud of the fact that some of his songs were used in the sound track for "The Trailer Park Boys," written and produced by Mike Clattenburg, son of Dutch's first drummer and best friend, Kenny Clattenburg. He was also proud of having received the Dutch Mason Lifetime Achievement Award, given out by the Fredericton Harvest Jazz and Blues Festival.

By the late 1980s, his lungs were already starting to give him trouble and he played less and less. He could still sing without too much difficulty but playing the harp became increasingly problematic. I only got a chance to perform with Dutch because Rick's health restricted his playing.

Next to Dutch, Rick was without any doubt the coolest guy any of us had ever met. He would carry himself like someone who just found out that their worst enemy had lost all their money. He had a walk that said—"I am here and you ain't." And he always dressed real sharp: black pointy-toed boots, green shark skin suit, hair greased back, and sunglasses that were dark on the top half but clear on the bottom. He had a look in his eye that was earned from tough living—enough to keep even Satan at bay.

There was not much you could throw at Rick that he had not already seen. There was the three inch scar that ran from his ear to his upper lip. Rick never told me all the details of what happened, just that he had been jumped in the shower of a motel he was staying at by someone he'd scammed in a drug deal. After Rick was knifed in the face, the two struggled for a while, eventually calling it a draw, shaking hands and making up.

Every time I played with Rick, friends would come up to me after and ask, always with both shock and hesitancy in their voice: "You know that guy? What is he like? Is he really as scary as he looks?" People could not take their eyes off him when he was on the stage. He would puff on a gigantic cigar, sending clouds of smoke over the stage, especially aiming it at Barry Cooke, because Rick knew how much Barry hated smoke. Rick did not have a great singing voice but he could put a song across because with drama and energy. They say that on television you have to make all your gestures and manners smaller than life whereas on the stage they must be larger. If so, Rick's performances were surely for the stage. The harp playing, the way he put across a song, the facial expressions were all extravagant and grand.

As we were driving to Yarmouth for the funeral, I told Carter and Barry what I'd told Rick's daughter Christine, to "tell him he's in my thoughts and that I love him." We all laughed because we knew what Ricky would have said if he were still with us.

"You're not trying to corn-hole me now are ya, Dave?"

Rick tried to keep up the front of the macho blues man. This was part of the image that blues players always try to project. Robert Johnson was poisoned by a jealous lover; Little Walter was killed in a fight on the streets of Chicago. The blues world can be violent, painfully misogynistic and homophobic. Rick Fines, the blues singer and songwriter from Peterborough, does not sing the lyrics to the Moses Allison classic "Parchment Farm" as they are written for this reason.

One line says: "I am here for life and all I did was kill my wife." Rick Fines changes the words at this point in a small protest against the sexism rampant in blues. Rick Jeffery also recorded this tune and did sing the words as written. When I asked him about it he said that yes the words are bad but that is the way they were written and after all it is just a song. Rick, the doting father, the devoted caretaker of the mentally ill, Rick the thoughtful friend was also the Rick who wanted his epitaph to read "Here lies Rick Jeffery. I never killed anybody and I never gave a man head."

CHAPTER TWENTY-TWO

Yarmouth

Sunday, November 30

Skin off my tattoos, knock out my gold teeth,
Skin off my tattoos, knock out my gold teeth
Went a way down in Mexico, so my soul can sleep.

I'm gonna miss my momma, but I'll go first I know
I'm gonna miss my momma, but I'll go first I know
Then I won't have to kiss her, when she's stiff and cold
(I can't do that momma!)

"Skin Off My Tattoos," Rick Jeffery

The funeral perfectly encapsulated the contradictory character of the man. The casket was open and we all commented on how good Rick looked. Appearance was important to Rick. He wanted to be the coolest and he was. When I went forward to view the body and say my last goodbye I brought a harp up with me. You do not want to let a fellow harp player go to the other side without a harp to play. I guess I was not the only one who thought that way. He had one in his hand. The altar had three large stands with pictures mounted on them. Some were of Rick as a boy, but most were of him in his days as a harp player, and most of these were of him and Dutch. Dutch was his hero and his best friend, and he looked upon Dutch's son Garrett as his own. Standing out were the photos of Rick with the stitches still in his face from the knife fight that had left him scarred. He had written at the bottom of the photo, "It ain't pretty, but it's real." I was especially proud of the picture of the two of us that was taken during the recording of the "AJ and the Red Hots" CD that Rick produced. Of course, that album wasn't the only time he was involved in the recording of an album. Sometime near the end of the tour, Ricky had been on our minds. As always, Dutch told the story best.

We were making Special Brew, down in Dartmouth. They said— "You've got to have a couple of songs that you wrote yourself," so I wrote a couple of songs, whatever the *f* they were. Oh, they were "It's All Wrong, But It's All Right" and "Trying To Find My Baby." Those were the two songs I wrote, but Ricky wanted to write them all, every *f*'n song. Ricky said, "I wrote twenty songs." I said—"You expect me to put twenty songs of yours on a *f*'n album?" "Well, they wanted us to write songs," he said. We had an argument about that. I said—"Ricky, we can't just make an album and put twenty of your songs on it." But he thought we could. I said—"Fuck, what does that mean? You can't do that"—but I couldn't get it through to him. Once he got something in his *f*'n head, it was like, you could take a nail and bend it over, you couldn't get it through to him. Finally, I just told him—"No, we're not doing that."

❊ ❊ ❊ ❊

Rick and Dutch are perfect paradigms of the blues musician. They ooze the contradictions that attract people to blues music and blues players.

Dutch always considered Rick his right-hand man because he was the true mirror image of Dutch. They both came from small towns in Nova Scotia. They both came from musical families. And they both wanted to live as outsiders, happy to experience the world from the ironic perspective of one who rejects the conventions of society, but who lives nonetheless according to the codes of a subclass. It's like a wolf pack, where there is deep affection and comradeship but also fierce struggle at mealtime. Rick was pretty close to the top of the heap, and he carried himself with the confidence of an alpha male...when he was in the blues world. When he was not Dutch's harp player, he was shy and painfully anxious. He retreated from what we now call "generalized anxiety disorder" by consuming unimaginably large quantities of drugs. Eventually he was able to get enough control over himself and his difficulties to get out from under that terrible weight. We often talked of our common struggle with anxiety and I was struck by the juxtaposition of the supremely confident bluesman and the friend who some days could not bring himself to get out of bed.

❖ ❖ ❖ ❖

Ricky was laid to rest on a cold November morning in his home town of Yarmouth. We gathered at Sweeney's Funeral Home, where a service was held in the chapel. He was buried in Chegoggin, Yarmouth County, NS.

His death was reported on television and radio stations across the country. He would have been very pleased to know that he was so well respected and remembered. Death makes us confront life. That we are not immortal gods, that our days are not without end, forces us to live with intensity and urgency. This passion can manifest itself as paralyzing anxiety and fear, but it forces us unrelentingly to face the question of who we are and what we want to be. You have to choose and every choice is both an affirmation of one life and a negation of many others. Rick and Dutch have paid a heavy price to be blues men, but in the end they have become what they most wanted to be.

❖ ❖ ❖ ❖

I thought after the funeral, driving back from Yarmouth, that only Dutch, the largest figure in Ricky's life and in so many other blues musicians' lives, was left to keep it all going on. Perhaps it's fitting that the leader, the patriarch of Canadian blues and of all the musicians who've played and gone before him, has outlived many. Dutch had stayed back in Truro, not able to attend because of his anxiety about funerals. He did attend a ceremony the next week in Halifax and I remember him telling me how hard even that was for him.

By Bridgewater, the banter about Ricky and his life with Dutch on the road quieted down and we were all left to our own thoughts as we drove into the night.

Mine came around for some reason to Garrett Mason. I remembered him on stage at Bearly's just a week or so before: the magic that he was pushing out of his guitar; the confidence of his vocals; the stage presence that must simply awe his father, because his father knows talent when he sees it better than anyone else I've ever met. It struck me that it is Garrett's time and place to keep the music alive in the Mason family—from the piano playing of his grandmother in church, to the Dixieland bands of his grandmother and grandfather, to his father's Dutch Mason Trio, to the Dutch Mason Blues Band, and on and on.

Dutch had only one seventy-eight rpm record to nurture his love of the blues, that B. B. King recording of "Sweet Little Angel" on the

Wurlitzer jukebox in his father's Kentville restaurant in the mid 1950s. Garrett has a heritage of blues to his advantage. He's learned all that from his father.

❖ ❖ ❖ ❖

Months have passed since the tour ended and Rick was laid to rest. I've had a chance to meditate on my experiences of being on the road with Dutch Mason and I keep asking myself what I've learned.

Many questions turn over and over in my head, but one dominates. Who is this man, this singular character, this legend and icon, Dutch Mason?

Listening to his stories, of his fifty years of living and playing on the road, and watching him perform during those three weeks, gave me an insight into the public side of his life. Dutch is a legend for his incredible feats of drinking, for the wild antics of his band. He is a man who could drink eighty, yes eight-zero, ounces of vodka in a day, on top of his regular dose of valium. He is someone who still chain-smokes during every single waking moment. I often wondered if he smoked in the shower. He cared so little for his health that one time, when playing out west, he noticed that his foot had swollen so badly he couldn't remove his boot. Rather than attend to it, he said ƒ it and just left the boot on until he returned home the following week. That was his first experience with gout. Simply put, he has the constitution of a horse.

I've learned that Dutch is Norman Mason, born February 19, 1938. That both his parents were musicians, that he grew up in Lunenburg and then Kentville. That he got the name "Dutch" because the kids in Kentville laughed at his Lunenburg accent. That he was good at sports and loved the cadets. That he was married three times and has two sons. I found out as well, although only after much prodding and annoying questioning on my part, that he has won just about every award and honour a Canadian musician can win, that he knows and has gotten drunk and played with just about every bright star in the blues firmament.

Most great religions and philosophies tell us that you can know the real heart of a person, who they are deep down, by finding out what they love. Van Gogh loved to paint. It shaped every aspect of his life. It shaped his soul so that everything else he did or felt was filtered through it. Most people are not so singular. They don't have that one, single guiding love of their life. I can't say if people who have it are lucky or unlucky. Finding out what it is for me was the real reason for wanting to go on tour with Dutch. As I reflect, I am reminded of the conversation I had with Carter when he chided those (me included I have to admit) who are taken in by the wild side of Dutch. Carter sees the love, the drive, the commitment to the blues as a deep truth that has shaped Dutch's life since he first heard the sounds coming from the jukebox in his father's Kentville restaurant.

Carter is right. The answer to the question, "Who is Dutch Mason?" is: he is a lover of the blues; a bluesman extraordinaire; someone who sharpened his skills on guitar, vocals, drums and keyboards to a razor's edge. Blues has been the filter through which he sees the world. I do not mean that he loves his family or friends less. It's that blues is a metaphor that infuses every thought and act. It is to Dutch and the others who have said "I do" to the blues, what religion is to the churchgoer.

The smile on his face when Carter or Garrett play the solo just the right way shows how much those sounds echo still. Charlie Phillips has told me of how Dutch would occasionally hum the bass line that he wanted him to play. Mostly he would leave us alone, but always the emphasis is to be on the feel—*Don't play too much, don't try to be too fancy or show off.* It's blues and blues is about feeling. Maybe that is why everywhere I go I meet people who tell me how much they love Dutch as a musician and a man. He makes them feel as he does.

So how do you end a story of three weeks that has changed your life? You leave the last word to the source of it all. As Dutch would say:

Well, good night folks. Thanks for coming out. Let's hear it for this great band. They are really working hard for you and they are a great bunch of guys. On piano, we have Barry Cooke. Let's hear it for little Barry. On bass, we have Charlie Phillips. Let's hear it for Charlie. On guitar, we have a great *f*'n guitar player and a great *f*'n guy, Carter Chaplin. Filling in for Brother Rick, we have Dave Bedford on harp. Finally on drums, we have Ainslie, AJ, Jardine, my oldest son and my right hand man. Let's hear it for AJ folks. He sure is working hard for you.

So, good night folks and remember, you can lead a horse to water, but it takes a strong *f*'n man to drown him. And wherever you go, that's where you'll be; and remember one more thing —I'm walking so be careful driving.

Good night folks. See you next time.

DUTCH MASON OFFICIAL DISCOGRAPHY

I only wrote two *f*'n songs in my whole life. And the only reason I wrote them was because the record company said—"You've got to write a couple of songs." So I wrote them in the Colonade Hotel in *f*'n Montreal. I said—"Give me a menu" and she gave me a menu and I wrote two songs on the back of a *f*'n menu in an hour. I said—"There's two *f*'n songs, so let's go in and play them." That was it.

But we made more albums, a whole load of them. I made a couple of albums with Kenny Clattenburg and Ronnie Miller, like *Live at The Candlelight Lounge*. And there was *The Blues Ain't Bad* and *Give Me A Break*, *f*, all kinds of them. I can't remember them all, you know. They're around some *f*'n where. All kinds of *f*'n things. I don't know…

- Live at the Candlelight Lounge
- Putting It All Together
- Janitor of the Blues
- The Blues Ain't Bad
- Wish Me Luck
- Special Brew
- Gimmi a Break
- I'm Back
- You Can't Have Everything
- Appearing Nightly
- Dutch's Sixtieth Birthday Tribute
- 2004 CBC Recordings

PHOTOS

Dutch as a long-haired boy in his hometown of Lunenburg, with a friend of his mother.

Dutch as a boy with his grandfather, Norman, one of the most important influences in his life and after whom he was named. The photo was probably taken in Lunenburg.

Dutch hamming it up in his army cadet uniform in Kentville in the early 1950s.

Dutch with fellow army cadets whom he remembers only as "Newf," (centre) and "Frenchy" (right), Kentville, early 1950s.

One of Dutch's earliest bandmates, Harold Boates, left, with Dutch on the right, in the mid-1950s. The young woman is unidentified.

One of Dutch's earliest musical configurations, with Zeke Sheppard on the left and Bubsy Brown on the right, in the late 1950s.

Dutch circa 1960.

Dutch behind the drums
in the early 1960s band
"Dutch Mason and the
Esquires."

Young, lean
Dutch on the
left with two
of his earliest
bandmates,
drummer Bobby
Marshall and
bass player Billy
Scullion, in the
early 1960s.

Dutch, 1979, during a
photo session for the
album *Wish Me Luck*.
Photo by Doug Ball.

The Dutch Mason
Blues Band
in an album
photograph,
1980. Left to
right: Gregg
"Fish" Fancy,
Donnie Muir,
Dutch, John Lee,
Gary Blair
and Rick Jeffery.

GREGG FANCY   DONNIE MUIR   DUTCH MASON   JOHN LEE   GARY BLAIR   RICK JEFFE

Posing for a band shot in the early 1980s at The Great Canadian Beef Company, Jarvis Street, Toronto. Left to right: Gregg "Fish" Fancy, Rick Jeffery, Dutch Mason, Gary Blair, Paul Brown and Ron Lepard.

The album cover for *Dutch Mason Trio At The Candlelight Lounge*, featuring Dutch strolling down Spring Garden Road in Halifax with bass player Ronnie Miller and drummer Ken Clattenburg.

Dutch in a bluesy mood on the cover of *The Blues Ain't Bad*.

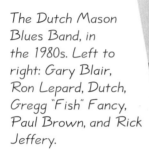

The Dutch Mason Blues Band, in the 1980s. Left to right: Gary Blair, Ron Lepard, Dutch, Gregg "Fish" Fancy, Paul Brown, and Rick Jeffery.

Dutch in Halifax during the late 1980s.

From the *Wish Me Luck* album cover session, shot at Montreal's Theatre St.-Denis, 1980s. Photo by Steve Aumand.

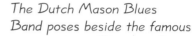

The Dutch Mason Blues Band poses beside the famous *Bluenose II*, docked in Halifax Harbour, circa early 1980s. Left to right: Gregg "Fish" Fancy, Donnie Muir, Gary Blair, Dutch Mason, Rick Jeffery and John Lee.

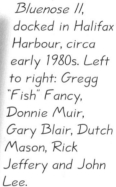

The Dutch Mason Blues Band in full flight at an unknown venue during the early 1980s. Left to right: harp player Rick Jeffery, keyboardist Donnie Muir, drummer Gary Blair, Dutch Mason and bass player Gregg "Fish" Fancy.

Dutch when he was still nimble with the guitar.

Dutch hams it up in Halifax with one-time band manager Stuart Gray.

The Dutch Mason Blues Band at Albert's Hall in Toronto, in the late 1980s. Left to right: Wade Brown, an unidentified sax player, bass player Dave "Soupbone" White in the background, with Dutch at the mic.

Dutch and his guitar—the epitome of the hard life of the blues.

Dutch poses in shades in the early 1980s.

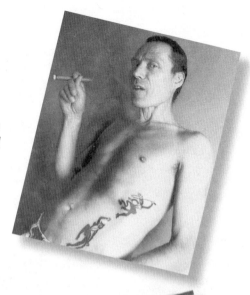

Rick Jeffery poses in the late 1990s for Halifax musician and photographer Morrow Scot-Brown on the occasion of his new tattoo, "Dancing Cats," a pair of feminine cat figures.

Drummer Ainsley "AJ" Jardine taking a break from a 2000 recording session in the home studio of Halifax musician Ian O'Donnell.

Dutch, centre, with friends Maureen and Dave Smith between sets at Bugaboo Creek, Fredericton, in 2001.

David Bedford, Ainsley "AJ" Jardine and the late Rick Jeffery at Bugaboo Creek in Fredericton, in 2001.

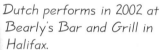

Dutch performs in 2002 at Bearly's Bar and Grill in Halifax.

Garrett Mason performs in 2002 at Bearly's Bar and Grill in Halifax.

ABOUT THE AUTHORS

David Bedford is a professor of political science at the University of New Brunswick in Fredericton. He began playing the harmonica in 1988, and by 1993 was sitting in with Theresa Malenfant. As part of AJ and the Red Hots, he has backed up blues figures such as Dutch Mason, Rick Fines, Rick Jeffery, and Dawn Tyler Watson, and has appeared on a number of CDs. He also plays in the Fredericton-based band The George Street Blues Project. David is married to Sue Tatemichi and has one daughter, Riiko.

Harvey Sawler began his career as a writer and journalist working at newspapers in Prince Edward Island and New Brunswick. Today, he is a regular contributor to *Saltscapes* and *Progress* magazines, and has published two novels, *The Penguin Man* and *One Single Hour*. A third novel, *Saving Mrs. Kennedy*, about American hero and Secret Service agent Clint Hill, is forthcoming. Harvey also plays drums for The George Street Blues Project. As a tourism and travel consultant, he exists in a virtual office—highways, airports and hotels—but is based in Fredericton, New Brunswick. Harvey has two daughters, Shannon and Vanessa, and one granddaughter, Maddie.